imaging

A SOUTH AFRICAN SCRAPBOOK

Andy Kempe and Rick Holroyd

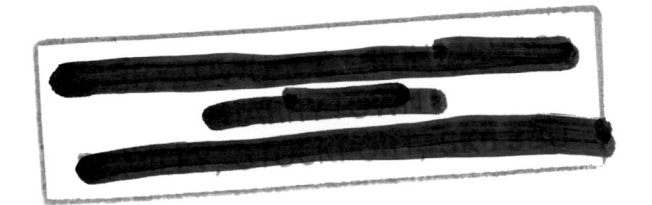

Hodder & Stoughton
A MEMBER OF THE HODDER HEADLINE GROUP

British Library Cataloguing-in-Publication Data

A catalogue for this book is available from the British Library.

ISBN 0-340-54835-5

First published 1994
Impression number   10   9   8   7   6   5   3   2   1
Year   1999 1998 1997 1996 1995 1994
Copyright © 1994 Andy Kempe and Rick Holroyd

All rights reserved. No part of this publication may be reproduced or transmitted in any form or by any means, electronic or mechanical, including photocopy, recording, or any information storage and retrieval system, without permission in writing from the publisher or under licence from the Copyright Licensing Agency Limited. Further details of such licences (for reprographic reproduction) may be obtained from the Copyright Licensing Agency Limited, of 90 Tottenham Court Road London W1P 9HE.

Typeset by Multiplex Techniques Limited
Printed in Great Britain for Hodder & Stoughton Educational, a division of Hodder Headline Plc, 338 Euston Road, London NW1 3BH by Thomson Litho Ltd, East Kilbride.

CONTENTS

Acknowledgements	iv
The Mathabes' story	1
A brief history of South Africa	7
Village life	11
The family tree	13
Life in the mines: Albert's story	15
Notice to strong boys	19
Albert in the compound	20
Albert's trial	26
Moving house: Lilian's story	29
Working under Apartheid: Katse's story	42
Domestic service: Florence's story	53
Black against black: Joseph's story	60
In Search of Dragon's Mountain: A play about South Africa	78

ACKNOWLEDGEMENTS

The publishers would like to thank the following for giving permission to reproduce material in this book:

Images:
Cover: Orde Eliason/Link; p 11 (top and bottom), Mary Evans Picture Library; pp 20, 36, 46 (top and bottom), 53, 60, (top and bottom), 61, 63, Mayibuye Centre; p 35, Associated Press; pp 38, 56 (top and bottom), 57, Orde Eliason/Link; p 52 © Jon Jones, Sygma; p53 © Peter Baasch/LINK.

Extracts:
p 12 'Unanana and the Elephant' from *African Myths and Legends* retold by Kathleen Arnott (1962), copyright © Kathleen Arnott 1962, by permission of Oxford University Press; pp 16–17 *Emakhaya* by permission of the International Library of African Music; pp 17–18 *Song of Agony* by Gouveia de Lemos; p 21 extracts from *Gold and Workers* by Luli Callinicos (Ravan Press, 1981); p 27 *M'Godini* (Shangraan song); pp 27–28 *Family Planning* by James Twala from *Gold and Workers* by Luli Callinicos (Ravan Press, 1981); pp 30–31 *South African police shoot white farmers* by John Mattison 12 May 1991, copyright © The Observer; pp 32–33 extracts from *Chain of Fire* by Beverly Naidoo, copyright © Longman Group UK Ltd; pp 40–41 from *Kaffir Boy* by Mark Mathabane, The Bodley Head; pp 42–43 extracts from *Journey to Johannesburg* by Beverly Naidoo, copyright © Longman Group UK Ltd; pp 48 'Trial puts spotlight on white violence' by Patrick Lawrence 19 February 1991, copyright © The Guardian; pp 49–51 and 64–66 extracts from *Waiting for the Rain* by Sheila Gordon, Harper Collins Publishers Ltd; pp 59 *Always A Suspect* by Mbuyiseni Oswald Mtshali, by permission of Ad. Donker (Pty) Ltd; p 63 *ANC targets the school crisis* 30 July 1991 The Independent; p 64 'Police shoot dead school protest boy' by Fred Bridgland 21 August 1991, copyright © The Telegraph plc, London 1991; p 74 'Threat to de Klerk as dirty deeds emerge' The Independent 26 July 1991; p 76 'South Africa quakes at prospect of civil war' by Allister Sparks 11 August 1991, copyright © The Observer; pp 78–82 *In Search of Dragon's Mountain* by Toeckey Jones, published by Thomas Nelson and Sons Ltd.

Every effort has been made to trace and acknowledge ownership of copyright. The publishers will be glad to make suitable arrangements with any copyright holders it has not been possible to contact.

THE MATHABES' STORY

INTRODUCTION

BLACK PROTEST ENDS IN VIOLENCE

RECONCILIATION OF WORLDS FAR APART

TENSION STILL GROWING IN TOWNSHIPS

MORE ARRESTS TODAY

QUESTIONS *to think and talk about*

- Read these headlines closely in pairs. Are there any words you do not understand? Which words do you know?

- What stories do you think the headlines could be describing? If you could read on, what kind of events do you think you would read about?

- In which countries could these events be taking place?

SCENE:	*A small room in a small house. The room is modestly furnished, but very tidy. The decoration is plain, but, again, well maintained. A man sits reading a paper in a chair. His daughter sits at his feet watching. She is very bored.*
SISSIE:	Daddy, why must you always read those papers? I want you to play with me some more!
JOSEPH:	You have your stories too, young lady. Can't I enjoy mine once in a while?
SISSIE:	But you don't enjoy them! I can see it in your face. They make you look so serious, and tired. I prefer it when you tell me stories. I like your stories. They even make you smile. But these papers, they make you sad. And they are so boring! I cannot understand them.
JOSEPH:	What don't you understand, Sissie?
SISSIE:	Well, the hard words. Like 'Reconciliation'. What does that mean?
JOSEPH:	Well … reconciliation is a … coming together, a peaceful bringing together of people or ideas. If two people have had an argument, for example, and then they make friends again, they can be said to be reconciled. A reconciliation has taken place.
SISSIE:	(*Reading*) 'A reconciliation of worlds far apart'. But what can that mean? If we all live in the same world, how can we bring two worlds together? How can there even be two worlds? We live in the same one, don't we?
JOSEPH:	Yes, we do. But it's difficult for us, very difficult…
SISSIE:	You see, you're looking all sad again! It is all these stories about 'violence' and 'tension'. Why is there so much trouble in our town?
JOSEPH:	Sissie, you ask such questions! (*Sighs*) The answers lie only in our history, a long, long time ago.
SISSIE:	You mean, when you were a child?
JOSEPH:	(*Laughing now*) Well, yes, I suppose so! But I did mean much further back than that. I am not *so* old, young lady!

SISSIE: Was there trouble in Grandpa's day?

JOSEPH: Yes, there was.

SISSIE: And even in his father's time?

JOSEPH: Well, yes, I suppose there was trouble then as well.

SISSIE: Always in our country?

JOSEPH: Yes, always in our country.

SISSIE: But the stories you tell me are all of our country – mother's are too – they never speak of trouble. I prefer those stories, The Magic Horns, Unanana the Elephant, Dragon's Mountain...

JOSEPH: (*Puts down paper*) Well, shall we have one now?
(*Pause*)

SISSIE: No. (*She opens the paper on the floor*) I want to know the answers to these questions.

JOSEPH: Well, I think that if that is so, you ought to read one more very special story.

SISSIE: All right. Which one?

JOSEPH: Well, it's this story. I've been wondering when would be the best time to give it to you, but I suppose you are ready for it now. It's the oldest book on my shelf! (*He reaches for an old tatty scrapbook*) I always intended to give it to you to read, but I suppose now is as good a time as any.

SISSIE: Why?

JOSEPH: Because I think that it will answer some of your questions about our country more easily than I can, that's why.

SISSIE: Who wrote it? It looks very old.

JOSEPH: Well, your great-grandfather did, and your grandfather, and grandmother. And yes, I suppose I had a hand in it too, as did all our family. It tells all our stories – it is the story of the Mathabe family, but in a way it is also the story of South Africa.

SISSIE: That sounds good, all about us. Is it as good as your stories?

JOSEPH: It's different. This is not made up, it's all true.

SISSIE: Well, can we start it now?

A South African Scrapbook

JOSEPH: Yes, if you want to.

SISSIE: I do! But only if you help me ...

A FAMILY HISTORY: THE MATHABE'S STORY
Life under Apartheid in South Africa

SISSIE: There's our family name, and our country. But what does Apartheid mean?

JOSEPH: Apartheid? That is another big question! You say it 'aparthate', Sissie. It means 'apart hood', or 'separateness'.

SISSIE: But what has that got to do with us?

JOSEPH: It is a way of ruling or governing a country in which all people from different races or backgrounds are kept apart in everything they do. The whites, the blacks and the people of mixed race in South Africa were made to live like this for a long time, and they were not been allowed to mix freely.

TASKS

South Africa is a country over 6,500 miles away from England, and it would take more than 11 hours to fly there in a jet aircraft, so it may be that you do not know very much about what is happening there.

1 Working in pairs, talk about the following points, and share as much information as you can.

– Where is South Africa?
– What do you know about it?
– Have you heard anything on the news about it?

You might like to try and locate South Africa on a class map or atlas. Put a large poster of the outline of the country on the wall. As you work your way through this book, you can record your thoughts about the various questions raised on the poster.

2a Now think about the definition of Apartheid that Joseph gives Sissie above. Working in pairs, note down ways in which people could be said to be 'different' or 'separate' in the same country.

b As a class, share all the ideas you have collected, and write them all up on the wall poster under the title 'Apartheid'.

3 In small groups, work together to create a 'snapshot' or tableau which would represent Apartheid to a stranger. Try to think of a picture which illustrates separateness, and capture it in a frozen image.

4 Again in groups, take ONE idea from your list on the wall, and improvise a short scene in which one person is separated, or made to feel apart, for the reason you have chosen.

5 Show a sequence of three or four incidents which would make you feel 'separate'.

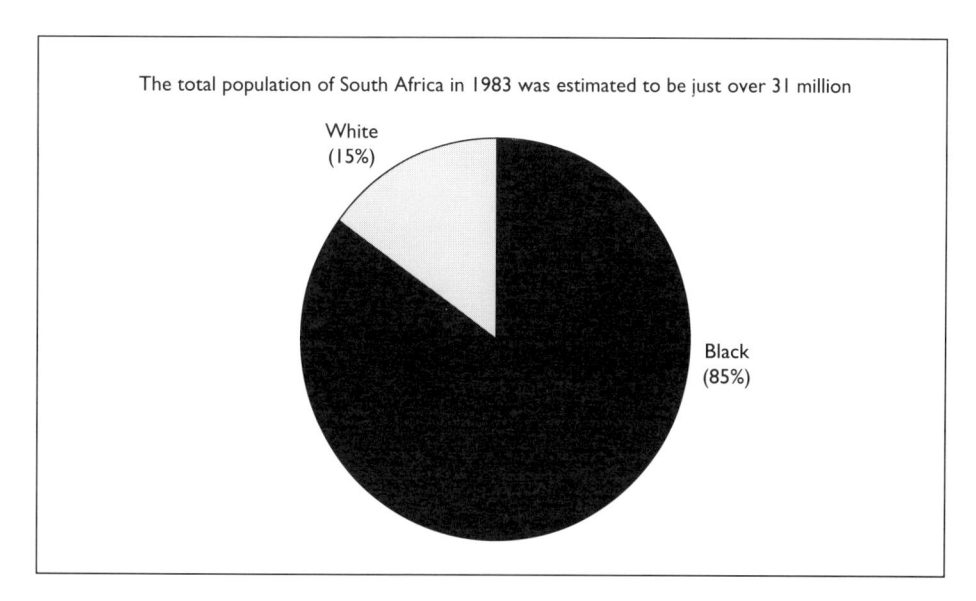

The total population of South Africa in 1983 was estimated to be just over 31 million

White (15%)
Black (85%)

Apartheid's most fundamental division was that of land. Whites were allocated 87%.

A South African Scrapbook

> JOSEPH: Now, look at the diagrams on this page. These show the numbers of the different races living in South Africa, and the way the land has been divided up. I cut these out of a newspaper and stuck them in some years ago.
>
> SISSIE: But, that's not fair...
>
> JOSEPH: Why not?
>
> SISSIE: Well, so many people, so little land...

QUESTIONS *to think and talk about*

In small groups, look closely at these diagrams. You need to know that the 'black' population of South Africa is made up of:

– Black Africans;
– Coloureds, or people of mixed race;
– Asians, for example Indian people who have come looking for work.

1 Do you find anything interesting or significant about these diagrams? For example, what do you think Sissie means when she says 'so many people, so little land'?

2 What questions would you want to ask about this country? Brainstorm as many questions as you can about South Africa, and share them in your group. Can you come up with any answers?

3 Think back to the word Apartheid. From what you know now, can you think about how all the people who live in South Africa were made to feel 'separate' or 'apart'?

Discuss your ideas with other groups in your class.

BACKGROUND INFORMATION

White people first settled in South Africa in the seventeenth century when traders visited the area. They soon settled when they saw how rich the country was in land, minerals and raw materials. Since then, there has been constant competition between the original black inhabitants and the whites for the land and riches of the country.

The system of Apartheid was set up in 1949 by the all-white government of South Africa, who decided that the best way to keep a peaceful and stable society was to keep the different races apart in everything they did.

The law stated that the whites, blacks and people of mixed race were to be kept separate in all places, including churches, parks, cafés, schools, buses, workplaces, homes and even on beaches.

The black people do not have a vote or a say in the government, and so cannot easily change this system, despite the fact that out of the 31 million people in the country, 25 million are black or mixed race. There are only six million white people in the country, but under Apartheid these six million held over 87% of the best land.

Many laws were introduced in South Africa to establish Apartheid, but they led to considerable opposition from around the world. This opposition has recently caused the white government to work hard to abolish many of those laws.

In the notes which follow, the names of the main Apartheid laws and the dates they were introduced have been given to help you understand the history of South Africa.

A BRIEF HISTORY OF SOUTH AFRICA

c. 800 – The first African native tribes, known as the San, began to settle in the area of Southern Africa from further North. Other tribes followed over the next 400 years.

1595 – Many Dutch sea captains began searching for a sea route around the African continent to benefit from trade with the rich spice islands of the East Indies.

1602 – The Dutch formed the Dutch East India Company to bring the spices back to Europe from India. But the voyage was a long one, and the ships needed fresh food and water half way...

1652 – The Company set up a fort with a small garrison on South African soil to trade with the natives, and to be used as a base to restock the trading ships on their long voyages to India. This was the origin of Cape Town.

1658 – The Dutch colonists expanded the fort to farm for their own profit, and started to use African natives as slaves to work the land, which was soon found to be agriculturally valuable.

1685 – Marriage between whites and non-whites was forbidden. The border of the original Cape settlement began to spread East.

1776 – The French occupied the Cape.

1779 – The first war with the Xhosa African natives took place.

1795 – The British occupied the Cape.

1820 – Four thousand British settlers arrived.

1836 – The Dutch farmers, angered by the British presence, left the Cape Colony to move North and East into the African country - the 'Great Trek'. Bitter fighting took place between the 'Trekkers' and the African natives (most notably the Zulu tribes) whose land they moved into. With the advantage of guns, the white settlers eventually triumphed.

1860 – The white settlers created the South African republic.

1868 – Diamonds were discovered and mining began.

1899 – Tension over ownership of parts of Southern Africa led to the Anglo-Boer war between the British and the Dutch settlers or 'Boers'.

1910 – The Act of Union was passed, uniting the British and the Boers in all-white control of South Africa. This led to…

1913 – The Land Act. This divided up the land for black and white ownership, with less than 10% going to the blacks.

1949 – The introduction of the Apartheid system by the white government.

1949 – Apartheid law: mixed marriages were prohibited.

1950 – Apartheid law: the Group Areas Act was passed. This forced single races to live in particular areas, which caused the compulsory removal of thousands of people to their 'homelands'.

1952 – Apartheid law: the Pass Laws were introduced, under which every black person over 16 had to carry an identity document to control movement.

1953 – Apartheid law: the Separate Amenities Act was passed, under which the different races were segregated in all public places (although the Act stated that facilities could be 'substantially unequal').

1956 – Coloured people lost the right to vote in elections.

1959 – Apartheid law: blacks and whites were segregated in universities. Black people lost the right to vote in elections.

1960 – Sixty-nine blacks were killed and over 180 injured when police opened fire on a crowd of protesters at Sharpville.

1960 – The African National Congress (ANC), a black group opposed to Apartheid, was seen by the government as a terrorist group and was banned.

1962 – ANC member Nelson Mandela was captured and imprisoned for opposing Apartheid.

1977 – Another black protester, Steve Biko, died while being held by the police – the forty-fourth person to do so since 1963.

A South African Scrapbook

1980 – The white government censored newspapers and reporting to other countries.

1985 – Pass Laws were abandoned.

1987 – Nelson Mandela was released after 27 years in prison.

1991 – On 1 February, President Botha announced his intention to dismantle the Apartheid laws.

1994 – First free elections.

QUESTIONS *to think and talk about*

- From the information listed above, and from anything you might already know about South Africa, who would you say the country belongs to? Whose land is it?
- Why do you think the early European settlers found it possible to gain control of so much land when they were so outnumbered by the native people?
- Why do you think so many Europeans wanted to settle in South Africa, despite all the risks at the time?
- Given that the government was faced with so many tensions in 1949 between blacks and whites, what are your views on the Apartheid system as an answer – effectively to keep the races apart in everything they did?
- Why do you think that the coloureds, and then the blacks, lost the right to vote in elections?
- Why do you think the all-white government decided to censor news reporting both in South Africa and to the world as a whole?
- What do you know about Nelson Mandela and the ANC? Have you heard anything in the news about them more recently than the dates given above? Find out as much as you can about Nelson Mandela's life in South Africa today.

The Mathabes' Story

VILLAGE LIFE

A South African Scrapbook

TASKS

1 Look carefully at the pictures of traditional village life. Can you think of any words or phrases to describe the people in the pictures, their work, or the way in which they live? Brainstorm any words which come to mind, and share them with the rest of the class.

2 Take up the positions of the people at work in their village. Take it in turns to say who you are, and what you are doing. Using movement and sound only (no words), present a scene to the group showing the way you work together on your tasks.

3 These are very much the scenes which would have greeted the Dutch 'Trekkers' as they moved out of the Cape area. In your group, imagine that the white people have been spotted for the first time. Improvise the meeting that takes place. How do you think the tribespeople might react?

As the native tribes of Southern Africa could not read or write, storytelling was a highly valued skill. This is the opening to a very old story from the Zulu tribe. It is called 'Unanana and the Elephant' and begins with a description of a village scene.

Many, many years ago there was a woman called Unanana who had two beautiful children. They lived in a hut near the roadside and people passing by would often stop when they saw the children, exclaiming at the roundness of their limbs, the smoothness of their skin and the brightness of their eyes.

Early one morning Unanana went into the bush to collect firewood and left her two children playing with a little cousin who was living with them. The children shouted happily, seeing who could jump the furthest, and when they were tired they sat on the dusty ground outside the hut, playing a game with pebbles.

Suddenly they heard a rustle in the nearby grasses, and seated on a rock they saw a puzzled-looking baboon ...

4 In pairs, read the opening and discuss what you think the story might be about. What do you think happens next?

5 Write your own version of the story using the opening given.

6 Gather the class around you, and retell your stories in turns to the assembled group.

The Mathabes' Story

THE FAMILY TREE

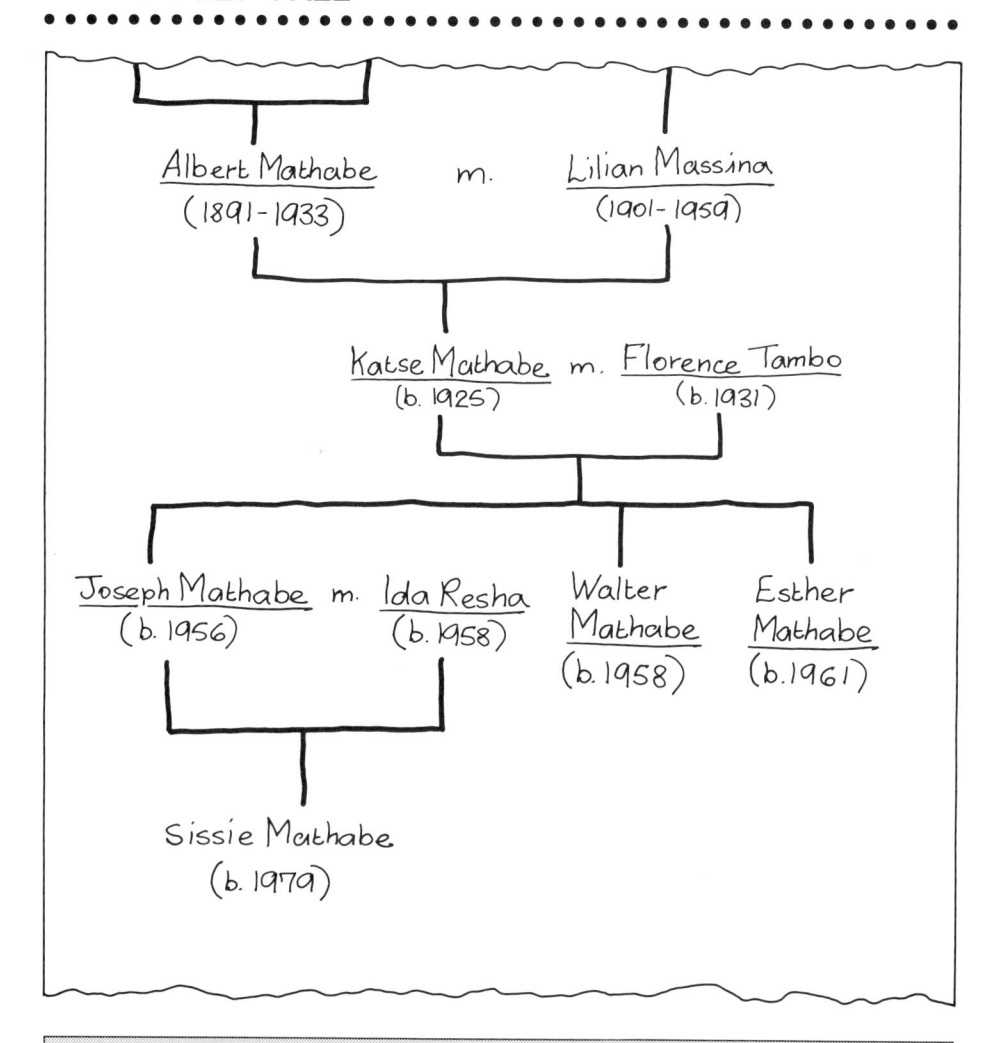

```
        Albert Mathabe   m.   Lilian Massina
         (1891-1933)           (1901-1959)
                    |
            Katse Mathabe  m.  Florence Tambo
              (b. 1925)          (b. 1931)
                    |
      ┌─────────────┼──────────────┐
  Joseph Mathabe m. Ida Resha   Walter      Esther
    (b. 1956)    (b. 1958)     Mathabe     Mathabe
         |                     (b. 1958)   (b. 1961)
    Sissie Mathabe
      (b. 1979)
```

SISSIE: There's Grandad Katse, Grandma Florence and Katse's father, Albert! Did he live in a village too?

JOSEPH: He did to begin with, yes, but not for the greater part of his life.

SISSIE: What happened to him, then? Did he lead a better life?

JOSEPH: Read on, Sissie . . . see what your Great-grandfather Albert has left in the book for you. He can answer your questions better than I can.

A South African Scrapbook

TASKS

1 Look carefully at the family tree. It shows only a small branch of Sissie's family. What is her relationship to the other people?

2 How many generations of your own family do you know about? In small groups, take it in turns to tell each other about the oldest relatives in your family you know of, or have heard about from your parents. Can you remember any stories about them to retell?

3 When you have shared these stories, try to think what life might have been like for these people. You might like to discuss these points:

– What did they have that we do not have today?
– Is there anything they did not have that we enjoy?
– Do you think that bringing up a family would have been easier or harder for them?

4 Try to sketch out your own family tree going back as far as you can. Focus on one of your oldest family members, and try to find out as much as you can about his or her life, work, home and so on.

LIFE IN THE MINES: ALBERT'S STORY

> JOSEPH: White Europeans settled in South Africa to mine gold and precious diamonds. They needed men to work in their mines, and great-grandpa was one of many men who left his village to go and work in a mine far away.
>
> SISSIE: But that must have been a much better job than just working in the fields, mustn't it?
>
> JOSEPH: He thought so, Sissie, at first...

BACKGROUND INFORMATION

One summer's day in 1886, two white prospectors discovered gold on their farm in the country area of the Transvaal. The gold ran underground for miles and miles, and the area has now been transformed into a highly industrialised urban mining area. It is the richest mining area in the world.

Setting up the mines, which required a lot of machinery and equipment, was very expensive and the only people who could afford to do this were the white Europeans who settled in South Africa once the news of gold spread. (This was despite the fact that Africans had mined gold on a small scale for hundreds of years.) The Europeans brought with them the money and the knowledge to control the mines. What was needed to make a profit was lots of cheap labour.

This labour was provided by Africans who often travelled a long way to work in the mines. Their way of life had been changed forever with the coming of the whites and they now needed wages for the first time to support their families back home. By 1899, after only five years of deep level mining, 100,000 labourers were employed by white mine owners.

The whites used taxes to make the Africans seek work – and wages – in the mines. A 'Hut Tax' was introduced whereby tribes had to pay one rand for each of their huts, and there was even a Poll Tax for everyone aged 18 and over!

Tax bills for Africans:

Hut Tax   = 1 rand
Poll Tax   = 2 rand
Labour Tax = 1 rand
Total   = 4 rand

Taxes had to be paid in cash, and the whites knew full well that, apart from working in the mines, the Africans had no other means of earning money, as this report of 1893 makes clear.

> Mine Managers' Report on the Native Labour Question
>
> 'It is suggested to raise the Hut Tax to such an amount that more natives will be induced to seek work, and especially by making this tax payable in coins only; each native who can clearly show that he has worked for six months in the year shall be allowed a rebate on the Hut Tax.'

This system led to a circle of poverty in which the black Africans became trapped: money was needed for taxes, so the men *had* to find work in the mines.

These tribal songs suggest how many of the workers felt about their new employment, far away from their villages and families.

> ### EMAKHAYA
>
> Go, let us go my friends, go home.
> Go, let us go to see our little hills.
> We've long been working on the mines,
> We long have left our homes for this, the place of gold.
>
> When we get home they will be waiting there,
> Our Mothers happy when we come inside,
> At Mazandekeni, home, my home.

Life in the Mines: Albert's Story

> Return my brother, from the place of gold.
> Reject the town.
> Cherish your mother, children and your own.
> They'll clap their hands for joy
> When you come home,
> At home where they are waiting.
> Come, come home.
> *(Zulu song).*
>
> The two of us Mother, will pine on the mine dumps.
> But we will meet again at the Ntombela Pass.
> *(Zulu song).*

> SONG OF AGONY
> 'Vê nerá, né 'Verá' cufä?'
> I put on a clean shirt
> and go to work my contract
> Which of us
> which of us will come back?
> Four and twenty moons
> not seeing women
> not seeing my ox
> not seeing my land
> Which of us
> which of us will die?
> I put on a clean shirt
> and go to work my contract
> to work far away.
> I go beyond the mountain
> into the bush
> where the road ends
> and the river runs dry.
> Which of us
> which of us will come back?
> which of us
> which of us will die?
> Put on a clean shirt
> it's time to work the contract.
> Get into the wagon, brother
> we must travel night and day.

> Which of us
> which of us will come back?
> which of us
> which of us will die?
>   Which of us will come back
>   to see women
>   to see our lands
>   to see our oxen?
> Which of us will die?
> which of us?
> which of us?
> which of us
>
> Gouveia de Lemos

QUESTIONS *to think and talk about*

- Can you think of any way in which the Africans could have escaped the circle of poverty? Were any other options left open to them?
- People have to pay taxes all over the world, but what do we pay them for? How much do you know about the money your parents pay in taxes? What is significant about the taxes charged to the Africans?

TASKS

1 Read the two songs again carefully. How do you think that the singers feel about their lives as mine workers? Which particular words in each song do you think make this feeling clear?

2 How do you think that these songs should be read aloud? Work with a partner and read the songs to each other. Which **words** do you need to stress? What **tone** of voice should you use?

3 How do you think that either of these two songs could be performed? In groups of four, work on a presentation which will include movement, shared reading and actions, and which will convey the feeling of the song to the rest of the class.

Life in the Mines: Albert's Story

NOTICE TO STRONG BOYS

NOTICE
To Strong Boys

I wish to make it publicly known that Sesioana of Maseru and myself have stopped flogging at Picaninny Kimberley Compound, Pretoria. Today it is your time to earn money. Wages are from 3/- to 12/- a day, according to your strength. I shall pay Hut-tax for you and shall also pay railway fares for you to Maseru to 'picanniny Kimberley'. I can also get good work at 'New Rietfontein' where you may receive wages from £3 to £6 a month. I shall also pay Hut-tax and railway fares for you from Maseru to 'New Rietfontein'. We have agreed together with the compound managers that if a person is sick he must be sent home with the Company's money and the railway fare to Maseru; they have thus bound themselves. Now my friends it is time for you to come to your friend in order to understand. The cattle have udders, come and milk them!

> 'We do not like our men to go to the mines because they go there to die'
> – Village Chief

SISSIE: Where did this 'Notice' come from?

JOSEPH: It appeared in Albert's village one day when he was just a young man. It was a sort of advert for jobs in the mines.

SISSIE: Why does the chief sound so serious? If the men needed the money for their families and to pay their taxes, he should have let them go!

JOSEPH: Indeed he did, and Albert was one of those young men. But mining was a very dangerous job, and the representatives sent from the mines to find new workers had to work hard to attract them. They were called 'touts' and were paid for every worker they could find. In one district, the touts were called 'dikalatsane'.

SISSIE: What does that mean?

JOSEPH: It means 'deceivers'.

A South African Scrapbook

TASKS

1a In groups of four, look closely at the notice 'To Strong Boys' which has appeared in your village. Imagine you are villagers reading this for the first time. What is your reaction?

b Make a list of all the questions you would like to ask the 'tout' about working in the mines. These questions can be put to a volunteer in the 'hot seat' who will take on the role of the tout in a village meeting.

2 The whole village gets together. Share your opinions with the other groups. Who wants to go and earn money, have free food and free housing? Who does not want to go? Why?

3 After the meeting, go back into your groups. What do you think of the scheme now? You must decide whether you are to go or not.

4 Reread the tribal songs on p.16–18. Imagine that you have heard these from other workers who have returned from the mines. What concerns do they seem to suggest about the mine work? Go back to the tout and challenge him with these worries. What is the response?

ALBERT IN THE COMPOUND

Life in the Mines: Albert's Story

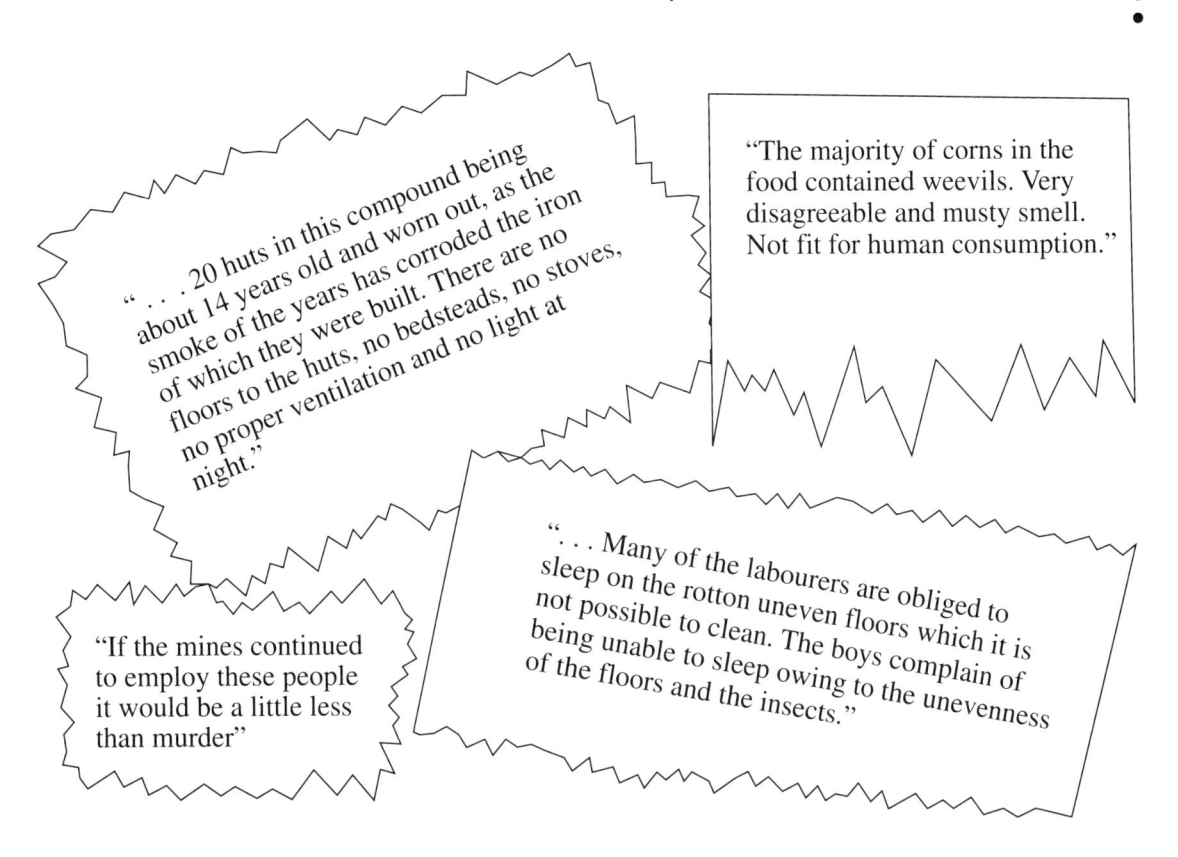

"... 20 huts in this compound being about 14 years old and worn out, as the smoke of the years has corroded the iron of which they were built. There are no floors to the huts, no bedsteads, no stoves, no proper ventilation and no light at night."

"The majority of corns in the food contained weevils. Very disagreeable and musty smell. Not fit for human consumption."

"If the mines continued to employ these people it would be a little less than murder"

"... Many of the labourers are obliged to sleep on the rotton uneven floors which it is not possible to clean. The boys complain of being unable to sleep owing to the unevenness of the floors and the insects."

SISSIE: Who is that?

JOSEPH: That, Sissie, is your great-grandfather, Albert Mathabe.

SISSIE: But the notice said they'd love it! 'Now my friends, it is time to come to your friend in order to understand'!

JOSEPH: As I said, they had to work hard to attract them. The conditions in the compounds where they lived were very different from what they had been led to believe. The life was very hard. In 1903 alone, it was reported that 5,022 men died in the mines from accidents, as well as from poor living conditions.

SISSIE: Is this the free housing that they were offered?

JOSEPH: Yes. The free housing was in the form of huge compounds, like prison camps, where the men were herded together. Conditions were filthy, and many men died of disease. There was even one idea to turn them into prisons with guards at the gate, so that the men could not escape until their long contracts, which were often for six to twelve months, were over.

A South African Scrapbook

TASKS

1 In pairs, look closely at the picture of Albert in the compound, and read the extracts from the reports of compound life. Share all the details you can think of which describe the way in which he has to live. Also include any feelings the picture suggests to you.

2 Now imagine that you are one of the following people: Albert's wife, Albert's brother, the mine 'tout', or a young man in the village who would like to leave and work in the mine. In your role, write down a sentence or two which you think best describes the conditions in the compound. Write on a large piece of card, at the centre of which you could place a picture of Albert.

3 Now share your jottings. Do they vary in any way? Call upon some of the authors to try and justify their words.

> June 10 1910
> ...First sight of our 'Free Housing'. We have concrete huts to live in with little space and no privacy. We sleep on cold, damp concrete slabs and the insects keep us awake at night... ...In our tribe it is against tradition that a son should see his father naked or on the toilet, but here we have no choice... life has changed all that...

> July 1910
> ...The food is getting worse. All our spare money goes on extra to keep us going, so we can send little home... We are given 5lbs of porridge a week and 2lbs of meat, but this is often rotten and the bread has maggots in it. Men spend all their money on drink to keep bad thoughts away. My friend says 'If one is not drunk, one is homesick...'

4 Read the extracts from Albert's diary which have been stuck in the scrapbook. What else would you like to know about life in the compounds? In small groups, question a volunteer who is willing to take on the role of Albert in a 'hot seat'.

5 Look back at all the words you have collected on the large sheet of card. Do you want to add any others as a result of interviewing Albert? Now try to make a headline out of the words. Imagine you are a journalist who visited the compounds at the time when Albert was there. Write an article on compound conditions which might have been published in an English paper.

6 Imagine that Albert's family have seen the reports on the mines. A member of the family travels to see Albert and tries to encourage him to return to the tribe. In pairs, improvise the discussion which takes place. Is Albert truthful, or does he tell lies about conditions to save his family from worry? Present the conversation to the rest of the class.

7 In small groups, act out two scenes from Albert's life, one before and one after he went to the mines. Show the different kinds of work and people he encounters.

> August 1910
> Monday: a bad day today. We began work at first light as we have to cut 30 inches of rock now or we will not be paid. At 7am a rockfall broke my friend's leg. It took us 2 hours to get him to hospital. Great pain. The doctor said he could not come until 5pm. My friend died at 4.50pm from loss of blood and much suffering. No doctor had seen him. There are so many like him...

> SISSIE: If things were so bad, why didn't they run away?
>
> JOSEPH: Well, you read what the compounds were like. They were really prisons with guards to keep the workers in. They would have been punished.
>
> SISSIE: What about a protest, or a strike, even? Why didn't they try to change the way they lived?
>
> JOSEPH: They did, Sissie ... or at least they did try.

POLICE INJURED IN VIOLENT CLASHES WITH MOB

There has been more trouble at the North RandFontein Mine today. Police and troops were called in to break up a violent demonstration which resulted in 53 arrests.

The workers have been on a 'go slow' for three days, over a dispute about pay levels. They claim that, after six months, their wages should have been increased from one shilling a day to one shilling and sixpence.

However, the owners point out that the contract states that while most workers will have their wages increased, that does not mean *all* workers. The 'Boss Boys' or team leaders have been offered an increase, but not the ordinary workers.

Last Wednesday, as reported in this paper, that offer was rejected, and the go slow strike resulted, with every man digging only the bare minimum of 13 inches of rock a day. The losses to the mine over the last three days have been huge.

As a result, mine police and troops were called in today to arrest the strikers. The men sat on a mine dump, and threw bottles and stones at the police. After two hours, police managed to arrest 53 strike leaders, who will be charged with 'public violence'. They have not broken their contracts, but this greater crime can carry up to twelve months' hard labour as a punishment.

The cases will be heard this week.

> SISSIE: Was great-grandpa Albert involved in this?
> JOSEPH: Well, he joined the 'go slow', yes, as did all the men.
> SISSIE: What happened to him?

THE NORTH RANDFONTEIN MINE
CHARGE SHEET

Name ALBERT MATHABE   Age 28   D.O.B. 4-7-1891

Compound Address Hut 27 Block 4A

Pass Number 4138677-D   Tribal Group SOTHO

Status Hammer boy- Face worker   Branch RAND WEST

Previous offences
Breach of contract - attempted return to home village Nov. 1910. Returned after missing six shifts.

Details of present charge
Breach of contract - organised 'go slow' on digging - organised protest on the mine dump - resisted arrest - stoned police - injured officer with a bottle thrown during the fighting - attempted to bring Lancaster miners into the dispute.

Recommended Action
Charged with Breach of Contract; Assault; Disruption; Resisting Arrest.

Signature *Cecil W. Brookes*   Date 4th May 1919

Life in the Mines: Albert's Story

> SISSIE: But that does not sound like the man you talk about! Was he guilty?
>
> JOSEPH: Who can ever tell? Certainly Albert went on a 'go slow', although his only crime was that he cut the rock he was required to cut. This is what he had to say in his only letter home about it.

My Dearest Lilian

I have been given permission to write to you to let you know that I am well and that you will not be hearing from me for a while. But you are not to worry, as I am being well treated and am quite all right. In my last letter, I told you about the pressure we are all under to join the 'go slow' – well, it has brought great trouble.

We have not broken any rules, as our contract requires us to dig a minimum of 12 inches of rock a day, and we were cutting 13. But the mine was losing money, and the police and army were called in.

I was resting with friends on the dump after our shift when they came for us. They said they wanted the leaders – but nobody really knows who started the trouble in the first place. Anyway, they tried to take Kufa and Shoitto, and a fight started. We were very frightened. The police were using sticks and they had guns, and the miners were throwing lumps of dirt and rock at them to keep them back. The police charged the dump, and I was so terrified that I ran away with some others towards the Lancaster mine to get away. We were stopped and arrested as we ran.

Well, my dear, it seems we are to be charged, although nobody knows yet what with. I suppose that I will be back to work in a few days, and even though it seems we will not get our rise, at least I can continue to save for you and the family again. I am sure the whole business will soon be forgotten.

I needed to let you know that I am safe, and that you are not to be alarmed if you do not hear from me for a while. I will be visiting you all in July when my present contract runs out.

Give my love to all the family,
I love you very much,

Albert
xxx

ALBERT'S TRIAL

TASKS

1 In groups of three, take on the roles of Albert, a mine policeman (who has been told to interview him about the incident) and an observer who will watch the interview and act as Albert's defence in the later trial. Improvise the interview that takes place. The observer should simply listen and take notes at this stage.

2 All the actors in the role of Albert should now get together, as should all the actors playing the policemen, and all the observers. Pick one representative from each group, and send them into the middle of the room to set up the courtroom.

These three representatives should now improvise the court hearing. They should take it in turns to interview Albert, with the policeman acting as the prosecution and the observer as the defence. Your teacher may act as judge. Pages 23, 24 and 25 may be used as evidence.

The rest of the class may call 'time out' at any point to stop the improvisation and to advise their actor how to proceed, fend off questions or to open up a new point. The teacher should wind up the hearing and announce the verdict.

> SISSIE: What happened to Albert?
>
> JOSEPH: He was sent to prison. From there he came home, penniless and a sick man. He was looked after by his wife, Lilian, until he died in 1933. He had a terrible disease called silicosis, which is an infection of the lungs caused by breathing in dust. He was forty-two years old. His only joy was to see his first and only child born in 1925. After his death, Lilian was left to bring Katse up by herself. It was very hard for her.
>
> SISSIE: All that effort, all that work – it's just not right.

QUESTIONS *to think and talk about*

- Joseph tells Sissie that 'it was very hard for her' (Lilian, Katse's mother). From what you know so far about South Africa, what hardships would Lilian have experienced, bringing up a child alone?

Life in the Mines: Albert's Story

- Sissie feels that 'it's just not right'. From Albert's story, what is your impression of the mining contracts? What do you think that the mine owners should have done to change working conditions while still making a profit?

- What do you know of conditions in English mines and factories during the first few decades of this century? Do you think that things would have been any better here for workers?

- What do you think would have been an English visitor's reaction to the African mines of 100 years ago? Do you think that such a visitor would have been concerned by the conditions?

Many poems and songs were written by the miners during their stay in the compounds, to help them to work and to remind them of their experiences afterwards. These two songs were written by Africans and remind us what conditions were like for the workers.

M' GODINI

I went to the country of Jona
I find men working underground.
Working with tools in their hands
The hammer and drills of the bones
To break rocks that are so hard
Working by candlelight.

Fire ! zzi; fire, zzi!
Bad luck! The holes are blasted
It kills men underground.

(Shangaan song)

FAMILY PLANNING

Row upon row,
Like winter shaken stalks of maize,
The barracks stretch from one
Miserable end to the other.

They strip off to their vests
Embalmed in a day's sweat.
Yesterday's tripe and porridge are
Hastily warmed up for supper again.

They slip into their stony beds,
Clasp their sweat reeking pillows
As if they were their
Beloved ones left in the homelands.

They look at their shirts,
Overalls, trousers, jackets – all ragged,
Hanging aslant on the damp walls
Like faded, dusty family portraits.

Portable radios are switched off,
Candle flames flicker and die,
Darkness and silence covers
Them all like a large blanket.
Alone,
They quietly succumb to sleep.

James Twala

TASKS

1 Sit quietly by yourself and read the songs. Think about what kind of mood they create. How should they be read aloud? How do they leave you feeling?

2 Choose one of the songs, and plan a group presentation. You can present the poem using any form of movement, tableau or mime you like, in order to convey what the song means to you as a group.

3 Again in your groups, think of as many words as possible that relate to mining, digging and hard labour. Plan your own 'work song' which the labourers might have sung in the mines to keep themselves going. Remember that the rhythm of the words will be important here. (You may like to use handclaps, percussion, etc.)

4 Work out a group presentation for your own work song, and perform it to the class.

5 In pairs, think how lighting and sound effects could improve your presentation of these songs. Make notes on how these effects could be used.

MOVING HOUSE: LILIAN'S STORY

> SISSIE: So where did Grandpa Katse grow up – in the village?
>
> JOSEPH: Yes, at first. But at this time the white government started to move black families out of certain areas to live together in what were called 'homelands'. Lilian and Katse were faced with this removal from their village.
>
> SISSIE: But that's good, isn't it? Then all the black people could live together in peace?
>
> JOSEPH: Should they have to, Sissie? If you live happily in one area with friends and neighbours, should you have to move? Also, the homelands were a long way away from the white cities in which many worked, so the journey to work every day took hours.
>
> SISSIE: But how can it be called a homeland when it was not their home?
>
> JOSEPH: Exactly, Sissie, exactly. Nevertheless, Lilian and Katse were moved to a new area. This was their new 'homeland', although Lilian had never been there before in her life.

BACKGROUND INFORMATION

- Until recently, whites owned 87% of the land in South Africa, and blacks were unable to own land in white areas (as the diagrams on p. 5 show). The land the blacks were given to live on was the poorest, most infertile land that nobody else wanted. This land was split into Bantustans or 'homelands'. The blacks were made to go and live in these areas, according to which language they spoke, even though they might never have been there before.

- Movement also took place in the cities. Each city was divided into areas for different races by the Urban Areas Act of 1937. Furthermore, many blacks were moved out of the cities under the Group Areas Act of 1950. Any non-white owning a shop or business in the white area had to move out.

- The blacks were moved to 'townships' in areas outside the cities. This meant that they had to make long and expensive journeys to work every day in the white-only city suburbs.

- Families were moved by force; to resist would have been to break the law and face imprisonment. Trucks carried families' belongings to the 'homelands', where they often had to wait in camps for the huts to be built. Bulldozers then moved in to knock down their old houses so that new buildings for the whites could be built.

> What hurts is being driven like an animal out of your own home town. I was born in Johannesburg and proud of it. Now they tell me I'm a citizen of an up-country state called Qwa-Qwa – I've never ever seen the bloody place.
> *(A taxi driver speaking to a reporter from the Sowetan newspaper in February 1981)*

- Between 1950 and 1973, the numbers of people moved to new areas were:
  - non-whites   110,000
  - whites   1,600

- By 1983, over 3.5 million people had been uprooted.

- The removals prompted disturbing clashes in which white groups resorted to violence to clear land they claimed was reserved for them.

South African police shoot white farmers

South African police shot and wounded four white men and arrested three others yesterday while restraining a gang of more than 1,000 whites, led by Eugene Terre'Blanche, who attacked a black squatter community in an attempt to drive it from land the whites claim is reserved for them.

The incident took place at the Goedgevonden settlement, near Ventersdorp, west of Johannesburg, home of Terre'Blanche, leader of the paramilitary Afrikaner Weerstand Beweging (Afrikaner Resistance Movement).

It underscored the anger many conservative whites have toward President F.W. de Klerk's plans to abolish apartheid laws that have reserved most land for the white minority.

The whites arrived at Ventersdorp in pick-up trucks and on horseback and burnt down several shacks before police arrived. Several residents were taken to hospital.

A spokesman for the Conservative Party, Andries Beyers, claimed police opened fire on the farmers as they stood between the two groups. 'Three farmers were wounded by birdshot while a fourth was shot in the stomach with sharp ammunition,' he said.

This is believed to be the first time that police have opened fire on white right-wingers.

Goedgevonden, which is on government land, is the subject of a pending court action.

One resident showed a reporter a business card that fell to the ground in the attack. It belonged to Piet Rudolph, the right-winger recently released from prison by President F.W. de Klerk after being arrested for alleged participation in several armed actions.

Police told a reporter that Terre'Blanche was drunk in the Ventersdorp police station.

Later, the whites launched a second attack, this time on squatters in Tshing, the black township of Ventersdorp. At least 10 blacks were injured.

At a meeting later with Adriaan Vlok, Law and Order Minister, who flew to the scene, the whites agreed to go home and await the court action.

(by John Mattison, *The Observer*, 12 May 1991)

QUESTIONS *to think and talk about*

- Have you ever moved house with your family? Share experiences of how it felt at first to live in a strange area.

- How would you have felt if you had been forced to move somewhere against the will of your family?

- What problems would a forced removal cause you and your family? Think about the places of work, shops, schools and services that you use close to your present home.

- What do you find of interest in the numbers of people moved?

- What other questions would you like to ask about the forced removals under the Group Areas Act? Share these in a small group and see if you can come up with any answers.

A South African Scrapbook

In this extract from Beverly Naidoo's novel *Chain of Fire*, a young boy called Tiro discovers that his house — and all those on the same street — have been marked out by the government for demolition. The residents are to be forcibly removed to another area.

'Come over here, Ausi Naledi! Look here!'

Tiro stared at the number 1427 scrawled boldly in fresh white paint across the door of their house. He was on his way out to the village tap to collect the morning's water. Drips of paint were still settling down cracks in the old wood. Lightly he touched the '4' and white paint stuck to his finger. His nose wrinkled with suspicion as he turned to Naledi, his fifteen-year-old sister. Even in the dimness of the house, fear showed in her dark eyes.

'Who did it, Ausi Naledi? We didn't hear anything!'

Naledi shook her head, silent.

Wriggling between them, their little sister Dineo stretched and jumped to the full height of her four years, trying to touch the paint.

'No, Dineo! It's still wet!'

Pulling the child gently away from the door, Naledi held her small hand as they ran out to the low mud wall surrounding their yard.

'That's the one!'

Tiro's eyes shifted up the dusty track of the village road. In the distance, coming into view from behind a house with a tin roof, was a man in yellow overalls carrying a tin and brush. A group of people was gathering. The man seemed to be backing away. Still holding Dineo's hand, Naledi began to jog up the track. Tiro, eleven years old and agile, soon sprinted ahead. With thin, strong legs below frayed khaki shorts he ran effortlessly. Large white numbers glared out from the doors of the other houses they passed. As they got closer, they could hear their neighbour Mma Tshadi's voice rising above the rest. Her large arms seemed to be sweeping the man backwards.

'Don't you touch my house! Don't you step on my path!'

'Intshwarele, Mma ... excuse me ... It's not my wish. It's the government's wish. The government "baas" says I must put the numbers on all the houses here.'

He pulled out some paper from his pocket, but quickly stuffed it back as Mma Tshadi thrust out her hand to take it. At that moment the sound of an engine caused everyone to turn. A blue car edged slowly forward from behind the small thatched and stone church building further up the road. Two white men, both in pale-coloured suits and ties, climbed out.

'What's the trouble then?' asked one of them with a brief-case

Moving House: Lilian's Story

under his arm. He spoke in English.

'This lady ... she doesn't want me to put the number on her door, baas.'

The man in yellow overalls seemed to stand a little taller, now that his 'boss' was with him. He even spoke in English now, not in Tswana. Slowly surveying the group, the man opened his brief-case and pulled out some papers.

'Don't you people know you have to move from here? The trucks are already booked to come for you in four weeks' time now. So that's why you must have numbers on your houses. Then the whole thing can be done in a proper, orderly way and there won't be any upsets.'

There was a stunned hush. Mma Tshadi was the first to speak.

'What do you mean "move from here"? These are our homes. We live here. What do you mean "trucks are coming"?'

Naledi's heart beat fast. This white man must be from 'Affairs', from the Government, but Mma Tshadi wasn't frightened to talk up to him, speaking his language with a heavy Tswana accent. Younger than their grandmother Nono, she was a large woman with thick square shoulders and with a voice which had always been loud. The man from 'Affairs' looked directly at Mma Tshadi.

'Do you pay rent to Chief Sekete?'

Mma Tshadi nodded very slightly. Underneath the floral scarf tied at the back, her face was taut, sharply chiselled like stone.

'So you're a tenant ... Well, if you don't know about the move that's not our fault. The landowners here, Chief Sekete and his family, were informed long ago and we've had no complaints. In fact your chief has seen the place where you're going. I even heard him say that it's better than here. So you must ask him, not us. Now, let my boy get on with his job painting up the numbers.'

He raised his narrow eyebrows as he looked over at the man with the paint.

'Hurry up, John. We haven't got all day.'

Quiet with shock, the group stood watching as the man in yellow overalls hurried up the path to Mma Tshadi's house and, first checking with the paper in his pocket, slapped a number across the door ... 1438. Then he made his way across to the next house ... 1439 ... and the next. Saying nothing, but looking grim and determined, Mma Tshadi set off, followed by others, in the direction of Chief Sekete's house. [...]

from *Chain of Fire* by Beverly Naidoo

A South African Scrapbook

QUESTIONS *to think and talk about*

- Why is the black painter painting numbers on the houses?

- How might this job put him in a difficult position?

- Why do you think that he 'stands a little taller' when his white boss arrives? What does this tell you about how he felt before?

- The way people talk seems to be important in this extract. Why does Mma Tshadi speak 'with a heavy Tswana accent' to the white men? What seems to be the difference between English and the African Tswana language in this extract? What does the word 'baas' sound like, and what does it suggest about the status of the painter? Why is he referred to as 'my boy' when he is clearly a grown man?

- Who do you think has the power and high status in this scene? Find as many clues as you can to support your view, such as the way people speak to each other, the way they seem to act, the possessions they have with them, etc.

TASKS

1 In small groups, reread the extract up to the point where we are told 'There was a stunned hush'. Adopt characters from the scene, and position yourselves in a tableau which represents your idea of how the group would look. You may wish to add additional characters in the scene as onlookers.

2 Bring the tableau to life, and improvise the conversation which follows. Do not feel you have to stick to the dialogue in the extract, but say what you think your character would have *liked* to have said.

3 We are told that the chief of the village knows of the forced removals. Improvise a second scene, in which the villagers go with Mma Tshadi to see Chief Sekete to ask why he has allowed the removals to take place. What is the outcome of this meeting?

Moving House: Lilian's Story

SISSIE: What is happening here?

JOSEPH: This is a photograph of a removal in another village which Lilian must have kept. You can see how the army and police were involved to make sure that nobody resisted.

TASKS

1 In the picture, the police supervising the removals are white. However, the labourers and truck drivers who were involved in the removals were often black.

In pairs, take on the roles of a black truck driver, soldier or labourer, and a white police official. The official calls the black worker in to his office to give him instructions for the removal of a village. The black worker has friends and family in this village. Improvise the conversation which takes place.

2 In small groups, improvise the scene in which the black worker arrives at his relative's or friend's house to inform them that he must help them to load their possessions onto the trucks. What do they say to him, and how can he respond?

A South African Scrapbook

SISSIE: Who are these people?

JOSEPH: This is a picture which was in the newspaper. It shows Lilian with her friends from the village on the day they were moved. She is standing in the centre with Katse behind her.

SISSIE: What are they doing?

JOSEPH: I suppose they were waiting for their transport. While they waited, the bulldozers knocked their village down.

TASKS

1 Look closely at the photograph of Lilian and the villagers. In small groups, recreate the scene of the four characters packing up their belongings. (You may add other family members if you like.) The characters could take it in turns to describe the possessions they are packing and they could also explain how they feel as they prepare to leave their home. Freeze the scene as a tableau.

2 Bring the photograph to life by improvising the conversation which might have taken place over the family belongings.

3 Freeze the scene, and try to hold onto one feeling or thought which might represent what each character was feeling at the time. Take it in turns to speak 'your' thought out loud to the rest of the group.

4 Stepping out of the picture, use that thought as a starting point for a piece of writing – either a poem expressing the feelings of the person concerned or a diary account of that day. Use the title 'Moving House'.

Moving House: Lilian's Story

> JOSEPH: Lilian kept an account of that day herself. She wrote it down as she waited for the transport and kept it ever since. It gives us some idea of how she must have felt.

'Moving Day'

Only four weeks ago we lived in peace. Then the news came that we had to go. So little time, but so little to get ready. Even last night we still hoped that the trucks would not come. Some even talked of resisting, of fighting, but when we saw the police and the soldiers, all thoughts flew from our heads.

It only took a short while to empty the huts. A young soldier from the Transvaal helped with our belongings. We did not speak very much, although Katse tried to stop him moving his mattress, and the young man looked tired and sad.

Now we have been left to sit among our belongings and wait. Already we have been here for many hours and still no sign of any relief from the heat. One sad thing – we have had to watch as the big wagons came to knock down our huts before our very eyes – the children wept and the women were silent. All that is left now is dust and rubble. We hear that new houses will be built for the white people, as they do not want what is left behind.

We are going to be moved to our native 'Homeland' – a place I have never known before but which I am told is to be set aside for our people. The land there is hard and we will find it difficult to harvest, but I have heard that we can get into the city on buses and trains, and so we may be able to find work. I hope this is so. Katse is growing up fast and needs ever more food and clothing. He is a good boy, and I want the best out of this poor life for him. There is still strength left in me yet to work in service, and in that way I can help him. I pray that this move is for the best...

QUESTIONS *to think and talk about*

- What do you think Lilian meant by 'so little to get ready'?
- Why do you think that the white people did not want 'what we left behind'?
- How do you think that the soldier who moved Lilian's belongings might have felt?
- What would you suspect are going to be the main problems for Lilian and Katse after their move?

A South African Scrapbook

TASKS

1 Using a volunteer to take the place of Lilian as she sits and waits, 'hot seat' the character to find out more details about her experiences of the last four weeks.

2 Using the information gathered during the 'hot seat' activity, write another diary entry from Lilian's point of view, either developing the memories of the moving day, or using details from any of the days leading up to it.

> SISSIE: Where did Katse and Lilian end up? Sometimes moves take you to better places, like Uncle Walter's new house! That is much better than his old one!
>
> JOSEPH: Yes, Sissie, we do try to move for the better when we can. But Lilian and Katse did not have the choice we might have now. In many of the homelands near to the large cities, people were housed in townships. Many families were squeezed together in quite a small space. Katse's new house was in such a township, but it was not quite like Uncle Walter's ...

Moving House: Lilian's Story

TASKS

1 With a partner, look closely at the photograph of the township dwellings. Imagine that one person arriving in the township has telephoned a friend to let him or her know of the family's safe arrival. How would this person describe the conditions on the phone, and what questions would the friend ask about the new home?

2 Your teacher will brief you on your new accommodation in the role of the agent who has organised your new housing. What questions will you want to ask? What will you need to know about the new town?

3 In pairs, go off and 'explore' your house and the nearby streets, and talk to the other pairs you meet. Imagine that one person in each pair is blind. How would the companion describe the surroundings to that person?

4 Go back to the housing agent. What do you have to report? Are there any more questions you now wish to ask?

SISSIE: All these people look so sad! And they're just standing around, as it they had nowhere to go.

JOSEPH: Well, Sissie, often there *wasn't* anywhere for them to go. The townships were cut off from the places around them, and there was normally some kind of control over who went in and out of them. Some of them were even surrounded by barbed wire, and on the wire there was often a warning sign, like this one.

WARNING

THIS ROAD PASSES THROUGH PROCLAIMED BANTU LOCATIONS, ANY PERSON WHO ENTERS THE LOCATIONS WITHOUT A PERMIT RENDERS HIMSELF LIABLE FOR PROSECUTION FOR CONTRAVENING THE BANTU (URBAN AREAS) CONSOLIDATION ACT 1945, AND THE LOCATION REGULATION ACT OF THE CITY OF JOHANNESBURG.

A South African Scrapbook

QUESTIONS *to think and talk about*

- Read the Bantu warning sign which greeted people at the township gate. Talk about these points in pairs:
  - Is there anything about the wording, the layout, or the style of writing which you find difficult or interesting?
  - Is it welcoming and helpful, or not?
  - Why is a warning necessary? Who is it aimed at and why?

> SISSIE: Did Grandpa Katse and Lilian settle in the township?
>
> JOSEPH: Yes, they did. Their address was a grand one: Hut 3a, Yard 5, Meadowlands. Katse went to school there and finally got a job in the city as a bus driver - you remember all the games he plays with you about that! But Meadowlands! What a name to describe such a place! Never has such a fine name been given to so miserable a street ...

BACKGROUND INFORMATION

The conditions in the townships were miserable for many families. Homes were often the most basic of huts, with no running water or electricity, and many families had to share the same tap. One African called Mark Mathabane wrote this description of the house he lived in during his eighteen years in the township of Alexandra.

One night, our dingy shack, which had been leaning precipitiously on the edge of a donga, collapsed. Luckily no one was hurt, but we were forced to move to another one, similarly built. This new shack, like the old one, had two rooms, measured something like fifteen by fifteen feet, and overlooked the same unlit, unpaved, potholed street. It had an interior flaked with old whitewash, a leaky ceiling of rusted zinc propped up by a thin wall of crumbling adobe bricks, two tiny windows made of cardboard and pieces of glass, a creaky, termite-eaten door too low for a person of average height to pass through without bending double, and a floor made of patches of cement and earth. It was similar to the dozen or so shacks strewn irregularly, like lumps on a leper, upon the cracked greenless piece of ground named yard number thirty-five.

from *Kaffir Boy*
by Mark Mathabane

As a result of the security around the township areas, the vast majority of white South Africans went through their entire life without ever seeing at first-hand the conditions under which blacks had to survive in dwellings such as these.

TASKS

1 Think carefully about the name 'Meadowlands'. What associations does the word have for you? Share all these ideas with a partner. Why do you think that this name has been given to Katse's street? Look up the term 'euphemism' in a dictionary. How could the name Meadowlands be seen as an example of 'euphemism'? Why do you think that the dirtiest parts of some industrial cities in England have been called 'Salmon Pastures', 'Mount Pleasant' and 'Park Hill'?

2 What else would you like to know about Katse's life in Meadowlands? Think up your questions in pairs, and put them to one person who takes on the role of Katse. Is there anything in the essay you do not understand, or which needs further explanation?

3 As a government clerk, you have been asked to advertise the area of Meadowlands to try and attract new workers to the city. Design a poster which might tempt workers to come and live and work in Meadowlands. (You could use the idea of the euphemism from Task 1 in your poster.)

4 In small groups, plan a 30-second TV commercial to develop the ideas expressed in your posters advertising Meadowlands.

A South African Scrapbook

WORKING UNDER APARTHEID: KATSE'S STORY

> SISSIE: Grandpa Katse did become a driver, but not of a train; he drove a bus!
>
> JOSEPH: Yes, he did, Sissie. Every day, thousands of workers needed to get to jobs in the city, and he took them.

BACKGROUND INFORMATION

Once the black population had been moved into the townships, those who had jobs in the white areas of the cities had to travel much further to their place of work. Trains and buses are still dangerously overcrowded at peak times, and the longer journeys add a great deal of time to the working day. In 1978, it was calculated that workers from the Soweto township spent an average of four hours a day travelling to and from work.

The African writer Beverly Naidoo describes a train journey in *Journey to Jo'Berg* in this way:

> It was rush hour when they got on the train to Soweto, and the children clung on tightly to Grace. There was no sitting space and it felt as if all their breath was being squeezed out of them.

Grown-up bodies pressed in from above and all around them. Some people laughed, some people swore and others kept silent, as the train lurched on its way.

At each station the crowd heaved towards the carriage door, people urgently pushing their way through. Naledi and Tiro tried to press backwards to stay close to Grace.

But in a sudden surge at one of the stations, they found themselves being carried forward, hurtling out onto the platform. Desperately they tried to reach back to the open door, but passengers were still coming out, although the train was beginning to move on [...]

Like all other public services, there were separate trains and buses for white and black passengers. A black person could not get onto a white bus, even if it was half full.

TASKS

1 Examine the picture of the rush hour train carefully with a partner. Share and note down any words or phrases which come to mind. Concentrate on how it must have felt for those on the train: the heat, the noise, the smell.

2 Join together with another pair, and share all of your ideas. Try to form the words and phrases into the line of a poem which has the journey to work as its theme.

3 Plan a group presentation of your poem. You might like to use movement and sound to convey the motion of the train (and the feelings of those on board) as it pulls away. How can the lines of your poem help you to do this?

> JOSEPH: The other work Katse did was during the day in the white suburbs. He drove a bus for whites only until the evening rush hour.
>
> SISSIE: Only white passengers with a black driver. It sounds silly.
>
> JOSEPH: Well, it was very serious, as Katse found out to his cost one day. Read on and find out.

A South African Scrapbook

18 August, 1962

I am still worried about today. I fear that it could bring much trouble for me. I shall write it down while it is clear in my mind.

I was on the whites-only route in the city suburbs. The work is pleasant as the buses are quieter than those for the black workers. At one stop, two black youths tried to get on. I did not notice them as I was taking fares, and it was only when the shouting started that I realised they were on the bus.

They were clearly not from the city – perhaps they did not understand – and they were only young – perhaps fifteen? The white man at the front was calling them terrible names. I thought he was going to hit them with his bag. The people in the queue behind were also shouting and trying to pull them off. All they could do was to look at me and shout, 'The bus is half empty, why can't we get on?'

I was confused and bewildered, I admit. There was so much anger and shouting. I really did nothing. In the end, the man got the help of another passenger, and pushed them off the bus. Somebody called the police from a nearby house. The white man then took my number, and said he would report me. The police arrived and took the youths away. They said there was a problem with their Pass Books.

Well, they were in the wrong, but I do not know what my boss will make of it. I did not let them on the bus – they just got on! Perhaps I should have done something, but I was angry too! Why could they not have had a seat? There were plenty! But I should know better. That is how it is for us. I suppose that is why I did nothing at all.

I just hope that it does not cause me trouble. I will try to forget the whole thing and just get on with my work.

To be quiet in this life is by far the best thing...

QUESTIONS *to think and talk about*

- Why do you think Katse felt that the incident 'could bring much trouble for me'?
- What do you think that Katse means by 'That is how it is for us'?
- Katse states finally that 'To be quiet in this life is by far the best thing'. What do you think he means by this? Talk about this incident – and any other that you have read about in the book so far – and decide whether or not you agree with Katse. How can staying quiet help? What is the danger of speaking out when you feel angry about something?
- Can you think of a time when you were too scared to speak out and kept quiet? How did that make you feel, and was it the best action for you?

Working under Apartheid: Katse's Story

TASKS

1   What else would you like to know about this incident? In pairs, work out questions to be put to Katse in a 'hot seat' session.

2   In small groups, think how the whole incident could be retold in a series of tableaux. Which key moments would you need to capture to make sense of the scene? Which facial expressions would you feature? Rehearse a series of four tableaux which will retell the story, and share them with the rest of the class.

3   In pairs, improvise the conversation which might have taken place between Katse and his white boss. Complaints have been received from white passengers, and the boss wants to know why Katse did not act more assertively to throw the youths off the bus. At the same time, Katse has to think how to tell the truth without putting his job at risk.

4   Again in pairs, improvise the conversation which might have taken place between Katse and Florence, his wife, when he got home. How does she feel about the possibility of Katse losing his job?

> SISSIE: Grandpa Katse mentioned that the youths could have been arrested under the Pass Laws. What were they?

BACKGROUND INFORMATION

The Pass Laws

• Under the law of 1952, every adult African over the age of sixteen had to carry a Pass Book to be produced on demand at any time, day or night.

• The Pass carried details of identity, trade and homeland, and showed where in the country the holder was allowed to travel. If the holder was found to be in a prohibited area, he or she could be jailed.

• In this way, movement for African workers was severely restricted. No African could remain in any area for more than 72 hours without special permission, and entry into white areas was made very difficult indeed.

A South African Scrapbook

- Police raids of whole areas to check Passes were common: in 1975–6, 381,858 arrests under the Pass Laws were recorded.

- Women suffered the most; they needed their husband's permission, as well as that of the authorities, in order to travel. In addition, in 1964 a total ban was put on the further entry of women into urban areas except on a visitor's permit.

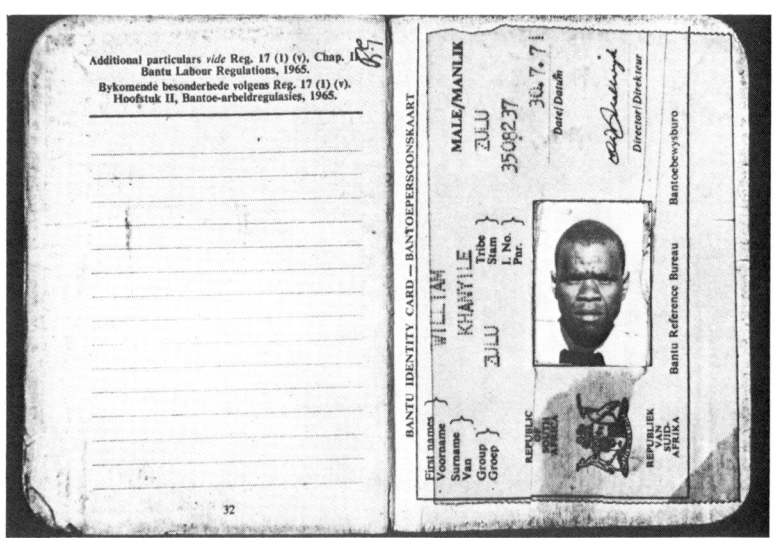

This picture shows the kind of checks that Africans came to expect. Despite the fact that the policeman is obviously younger than the African, he would have referred to him as 'boy' and the African would have called the policeman 'baas' (meaning boss).

The official language of the white South Africans is Afrikaans (derived from the Dutch of the early settlers). Many Afrikaans words and phrases used in conversation make strong suggestions about the relationship between blacks and whites.

Afrikaans words used towards black people include:

- kaffir — unbeliever
- domkop — stupid head
- piccanin — a black child
- skellums — rascals
- boy — the English word, which is insulting to elderly blacks

Whites who sympathise with the blacks are derided as being:

- kaffir boetie — little brother of the kaffir

Africans will normally refer to white people as:

- baas — master, boss
- groot baas — big master
- klienbaas — little boss, when the white master is a child
- madam — female boss

The following story is from an English newspaper and reports how a group of white students beat an African to death. The story illustrates some of the uses of the terms given above.

A South African Scrapbook

Trial puts spotlight on white violence

[…] In the Eastern Cape, four white schoolboys have pleaded guilty to culpable homicide arising from the death of a 70-year-old black man during a 'kaffir-bashing' expedition.

The boys, former pupils at Dale College, one of South Africa's best-known schools, were originally charged with murder. They also pleaded guilty to two counts of assault relating to beatings they gave to black men found on or near the school grounds in King William's Town.

The court heard that all four boys – 18-year-old Richard Bester and three juveniles – were members of the 'Frank Joubert Kaffir-Bashing Society'. They were boarders at the Frank Joubert Hostel last year, when their victim, Tom Ruiters, was beaten to death.

Exhibits before the court include a baseball bat, a truncheon, a hockey stick, a knuckle-duster, hunting knives, stockings (used as masks) and bloodstained clothes.

According to one of the state witnesses – a Dale College schoolboy who joined the kaffir-bashing society by signing a membership book – Mr Ruiters, a slightly-built man, was sleeping on the far side of the school fence when he was discovered by the kaffir-bashers.

Mr Ruiters, who reportedly 'reeked of alcohol', was thrown over the fence on to the school grounds and then dragged out of sight of nearby school hostels and houses, the former schoolboy said. Mr Ruiters was dragged to a hut and hit with an assortment of weapons and kicked on the head.

Another boy who testified for the prosecution told how Mr Ruiters pleaded for his life in Afrikaans. 'No, boss,' Mr Ruiters implored. 'I am not a kaffir. I am a coloured.' Bester's response was a kick to the head and the retort: 'I hate you all.'

The headmaster of Dale College, Malcolm Andrew, said the well-built Bester was a boy with strong leadership qualities. The school matron, Jean Kekewich, found him polite and helpful.

Several witnesses recalled that Mr Andrew had told the boys that they should take a 'two-by-four' plank to any vagrants they found on the school grounds. His remarks were made during a school assembly, the witnesses said.

Mr Andrew denied that he encouraged boys to assault vagrants on school property. His statement was made after the school squash courts had nearly burnt down and he meant to enlist the help of the boys, armed with 'two-by-fours', only in extreme circumstances, he said.

He did not know about the Frank Joubert Kaffir-Bashing Society. He did not regard any of the boys in the dock as problem pupils and was amazed to hear about their involvement in the assault on Mr Ruiters.

The trial comes in the wake of a controversial sentence in the case of a black man who was scalded to death after he had been pushed into a steam cleaning machine. His white assailants, Kenneth Westermeyer and his nephew, Johannes Westermeyer, were found guilty of assault and fined R500 and R200 respectively.

(by Patrick Laurence, *The Guardian*, 19 February 1991)

Working under Apartheid: Katse's Story

QUESTIONS *to think and talk about*

- Using the information on the Afrikaans language given above, think about what a 'kaffir-bashing' society might be. What attitudes towards black people does it suggest to you?
- Why do you think that the boys, in their defence, wanted to claim that Mr Ruiters 'reeked of alcohol'?
- Why do you think that Mr Ruiters pleaded for his life in Afrikaans? Why did he want to draw attention to being a coloured, rather than a black person?
- Who do you think the headmaster was referring to when he talked to the boys about 'vagrants'?
- What does the use of language by the whites in this report tell us about their attitudes towards all the non-white African races?

The following extract is from a story by Sheila Gordon called *Waiting for the Rain*. It tells the story of two boys – Tengo (who is black) and Frikkie (who is white) – who grow up as friends. In this extract, Tengo is at Frikkie's farm, where a family party is being held. Sissie is one of Frikkie's relatives, and Ezekiel and Selina are black servants.

[...]
Sissie came in pink-cheeked and hot from the dancing and excitement, with two giggling girl cousins, each carrying a plate with a slice of birthday cake on it. 'Ma says I have to have a rest, Selina. We're going to eat our cake in my room.'

At that moment Frikkie dashed in with a milk jug in his hand. 'My ma wants more milk for the coffee, Selina.' In his haste he bumped into one of the girls, dropping the jug and knocking the plate out of her hand.

'Oh, *Frikkie* ... Look what you've done!' Sissie exclaimed.

On the floor lay a mass of smashed crockery and squashed cake; pink and white icing was splattered over the linoleum and little silver balls scattered all about.

Tengo had been in the pantry stacking clean plates on the shelf when he heard the crash and tinkle of breaking china. He came to the pantry door and looked out to see what had happened.

'*Frikkie*, you're going to get it from Tant Sannie!' One of the cousins – a fat girl with a short, straight-cut dark fringe – held her hand over her wide-open mouth and stared accusingly at Frikkie.

'Oh, it doesn't matter,' the other cousin said. She was a thin, freckled girl of twelve, with a mass of red, frizzy hair. 'The boy can clean it up.' She turned to old Ezekiel. 'Hey, boy – Jim – what's-your-name, come over here and wipe this mess up off the floor.'

Tengo found that he had got from the pantry door to the middle of the kitchen without being aware he had moved. The shock of the girl's words had propelled him across the room as if he had been catapulted. He found himself standing in front of her, shaking with an intensity of hot rage that for a moment choked him and made it impossible for him to speak. He could not believe what his ears had heard – a strange girl addressing the respected old Ezekiel as if he were one of the stray farm dogs.

In a tight, low, terrible voice, Tengo spoke the words that came to him then. '*Don't you call that old man boy.*' He took a step toward her. '*You have no respect!*' His voice rose as he felt pure anger surge through him. 'Can't you see! He is one of the elders of our tribe – he is older than the oubaas – he is from the chief's family! *Who says you can talk to him like that –*' He lifted his hand as though to strike her, and his voice dropped as he hissed at her through clenched teeth. 'Don't you *ever* call an old man *boy* again.'

There was silence in the kitchen. From a leaky tap a falling drop dripped, dripped, dripped, plopping into the water in the sink. Tengo's mother stood still, filled with misgivings, her hands in the soapy water, watching over her shoulder what was happening. Old Ezekiel, facing them, wiped the plate in his hand over and over, turning it, dry and shiny, around and around in the dishcloth, a small painful smile on his face.

Tengo felt his heart lunge in his chest, pounding against his ribs and knocking his wind out so that it was hard for him to breathe. His mouth was dry, and he could hear himself panting. His fists were fiercely clenched and he stared at the girl.

Frikkie stood silent, baffled, shocked at the force of Tengo's anger.

The red-haired girl had drawn back, a look of fear and disbelief on her face. She had turned pale, and the freckles stood out against her blanched features. Now, in a sudden movement, she stuck her head forward on her thin neck. 'Don't you *dare* talk to me like that' – she spat her words out – 'You're nothing but a cheeky kaffir –'

Selina hurried forward, her hands dripping. 'Quiet, children. You mustn't quarrel. Don't make a fuss. It's nothing.' She came between Tengo and the red-haired girl so that they each had to move back. 'Girls, just go to Miss Sissie's room. Kleinbaas Frikkie, you go out and get another slice of cake for your cousin.' With outspread arms she herded the girls to the door.

'Tengo, I'm going to tell my aunt you've been cheeky,' Sissie called out over her shoulder, her face full of glee and malice. 'I'm sure my uncle will *beat* you with his *sjambok*!' Giggling, she ran off down the passage. [...]

from *Waiting for the Rain* by Sheila Gordon

QUESTIONS *to think and talk about*

- What are the most common insults used among your friends? How do you think people would feel if these were used towards them all the time?
- How do you imagine black people feel when the Afrikaans terms mentioned above are applied to them all the time?
- In the extract from *Waiting for the Rain*, what do the white girls seem to think about the old black servant? How is this shown in the language they use?
- Why is Tengo so angry? How do you think you would feel in his place?
- How do you feel towards the white girls? Do they have a right to speak to servants as they please?

JOSEPH: I remember the story behind this next picture. The Pass Laws even stated that, although a marathon runner did not have to carry a Pass while out running, a photocopy would have to be made and stuck to his vest in case he was stopped! This man was arrested in a white suburb for not carrying a copy of his Pass, and he had only been out running. The story got into the newspapers.

A South African Scrapbook

TASKS

1 In pairs, and using the examples of Afrikaans given on p.47, improvise a conversation in which a white person addresses a black servant. The conversation may be about anything you choose, but try to use the language to show who is in control.

  Reverse the roles and improvise the same conversation. Now discuss your responses to the conversations with your partner. How did it feel to act in each role?

2 Look closely at the photograph of the Pass Check on p.46. In pairs, improvise the conversation which might have taken place between the police and the male worker. You may wish to experiment with some of the language on p.47.

— Why was the person stopped in the first place?
— What sort of questions will be asked?
— What will be the outcome of your conversation?

3 *The Story Behind The Picture*. As local newspaper reporters, the picture of the runner has landed on your desk after his release from the police station. You are sent to research the story. In pairs, decide whom you will need to interview. Draw up a list, with some questions for each person.

  As a whole class, 'hot seat' each character in turn, using volunteers from the class. What can they tell you about what happened?

  Back in pairs, interview a township resident who claims to have further information about the runner or the incident. Make notes on what this person has to say. Does it match up with what you already know?

  Using these notes, write:
(a) an anonymous statement of the incident for the police records;
(b) the story for your paper;
  You will have to decide whose side you are on before you plan how to retell the story, as you cannot upset your readers!

DOMESTIC SERVICE: FLORENCE'S STORY

SISSIE: Wow! Is that where Katse lived when he married Grandma Florence?

JOSEPH: No, Sissie, not quite! This is where Florence worked in the city. She was a house maid and nanny to the Clarke family. She sent this picture in her first letter home to Katse.

SISSIE: Why did she have to write to him?

JOSEPH: Because often the family would need her to stay at their house, and so she would be gone from our home for long periods. It was often like that when I was a child.

A South African Scrapbook

My Dearest Katse,

I have arrived at last. The journey was so long and hot. All the buses and trains seemed to be full, it took me several hours. I do not think I will be able to travel home often. You will understand, I know. I have been given a small room in a hut down the garden to stay in, so you must not worry.

The house is so beautiful! The Clarkes are very rich and own a house with many rooms. The gardens are very wide and open with lots of trees. They even have their own pool. When I think what our poor Joseph has to enjoy at home! They are quite nice to me, and my duties are mainly cleaning and cooking.

Sometimes I have to take their children out. We have been to the park and the beach. These are for whites only — it makes me so angry — do you know that I am allowed on the beach only if I am minding the children, and I can only go into the water if the children get into difficulty. Only then am I good enough to bathe in God's good water! One black maid went to play in the water with her white charges, and do you know? the police came to take her away. Somebody had complained! The official actually said that 'white children would be faced with a real prospect of fraternising with Africans who will swamp our beach fronts'. Our beaches indeed. What a nonsense!

Anyway, my job is a good one, so I am going to stay out of trouble. The old maid, Sarah, was given the sack for having time off to return to the township. Mrs Clarke told me that she was always having time off for a funeral or something, so I don't want to fall in the same trouble!

So, I do not think that I will be able to get home for some time. There are house guests coming from England for a long stay, and Mrs Clarke has given me so much to do in preparation. I know you will understand, Katse, and we do need the money. How is Joseph? Ask Ruth if she will look after him a little longer until I can get home. I will save some money to pay her. He must keep up his studies! I know that you will see that he does, and Ruth is good, she reads to him every day, I know.

I must go now, there is so much to do. Sleep well, my dear, and look after our little boy. I miss you both very much and will soon fly home to you!

With much love to you both.

Florence

TASKS

1 In pairs, look closely at the picture of the Clarkes' house. How would you describe this to someone who had not seen it? What type of decoration and furnishings would you expect to find inside? Describe one chosen room to each other.

2 As an estate agent for Rand Properties, you have been asked to advertise, price and sell the family home. Again in pairs, explore the inside of the house, the gardens and the grounds and fill in the details on the Rand Property Sheet which will be given to you.

3 Back at the office, using the information given, write a description of the house of no more than 100 words for the advert. Your teacher will have some ideas as to the style of language you could use to do this successfully.

4 Look back at the photograph of the township dwellings on p.41. As more and more workers answer the adverts for work in the city, there is now a greater demand for housing. Fill in a second sheet for a township dwelling, using the information on pp.40–41. Your task here is to describe the township dwelling to a possible buyer without putting them off. Which details should you include and which should you leave out? (You may wish to experiment with euphemisms again!)

5 In the role of Katse, imagine that you have just read Florence's letter. What are your reactions to what she has said, her working conditions, and the incident at the beach? Write back to her, giving your responses, and telling her your news from home.

Domestic Service: Florence's Story

SISSIE: Things sounded very different in the white area of the city. Were all these pictures taken there too?

JOSEPH: Yes. Over the months Florence was away, she sent lots of photographs to us to show us what life was like for the children there. Katse and I used to cut them out and stick them next to the pictures we had of the township.

SISSIE: Why couldn't the black people just go and use the nice places? There doesn't look as if there is anybody to stop them.

JOSEPH: Well, to strengthen Apartheid, the government introduced an act called the Separate Amenities Act which reserved certain facilities for whites only. There were separate cinemas, cafés, buses, parks, beaches and even churches for blacks and for whites. Blacks could clean a white church, but could not pray in it. In case anyone should forget, there were plenty of signs to remind them just who the shops, parks, pools or whatever belonged to. Fortunately, these signs have been taken down now as the law has been abolished.

A South African Scrapbook

Domestic Service: Florence's Story

> SISSIE: It wasn't fair.
>
> JOSEPH: No, Sissie, it wasn't. I felt the same as you when I first saw these pictures. At school we read a poem about them. I brought it home for Grandpa Katse to stick in our book.

I saw as a child . . .

I saw as a child
A large advertisement-placard building
With refreshments and meals,
And I never knew why
While it was a restaurant
I was excluded

I saw as a child
A large beautiful space
With children and playing facilities,
And I never knew why while it was a park,
I was excluded.

I saw as a child . . .

A South African Scrapbook

TASKS

1 Look carefully at the photographs of the separate amenities. In what ways do the facilities differ? In pairs, list all the differences you can spot between them.

Again in pairs, think about the effect that growing up in these surroundings might have upon children. Share your views.

2 What other areas or places do you think black children might have been excluded from? Jot these down in a list, and then, taking two or three examples, try to use them as the basis for further verses to add to the poem 'I Saw as a Child'. Try to stick to the same style and layout if you can.

3 In her letter, Florence mentioned that there were English guests arriving at the Clarkes' house. In groups, decide who these people might be. Give them names and identities, and decide what their relationship to the Clarkes might be.

Set out the space as one area of the Clarkes' house (perhaps the veranda as shown in the photograph on p.53). Half of the group should take on the roles of the visitors, and the other half should be members of the Clarke family. Improvise the conversation which might have taken place at their first meeting.

Halt the improvisation. Imagine the visitors have seen some of the separate amenities on their way from the airport. What will their reaction be? The visitors will need to discuss this before the improvisation begins again. The guests now question the Clarkes about this policy. How can the Clarkes defend it?

Florence would have heard all of this! Imagine that she now writes home to tell Katse about the conversation. What does she remember about the conversation, and how does she feel towards the visitors?

> SISSIE: It must have been terrible. Just think how all those signs would have made you feel!
>
> JOSEPH: Quite, Sissie. Many people have felt the same way. There is another poem which I read when I was studying. I think it answers that very question: how did black people feel?

Domestic Service: Florence's Story

ALWAYS A SUSPECT

I get up in the morning
and dress up like a _____ –
A white shirt, a tie and a suit.

I walk into the street
to be met by a man
who tells me to 'produce'.
I show him
the document of my _____
to be _____ and given the nod.

Then I enter the foyer of a building
to have my way barred by a commissionaire.
'What do you want?'

I _____ the city pavements
side by side with _____
Who shifts her handbag
from one side to the other,
and looks at me with _____ that say
'Ha! Ha! I know who you are;
beneath those _____ clothes
ticks the heart of a _____.

Mbuyiseni Oswald Mtshali

TASKS

1 Certain words in this poem have been left out. Read the poem carefully with a partner, and see if you can guess what the words might be.

2 In small groups, rehearse a dramatised reading of the poem. Each verse should be represented by a tableau, which should clearly illustrate the incidents and reactions encountered by the black speaker. These tableaux can then be used to accompany a reading of the poem to the rest of the class.

3 'Hot seat' the speaker of the poem. What else can you discover about his life, his feelings about himself and the world in which he has to live?

4 Taking the viewpoint of *any* black character you have met in the scrapbook so far, write another poem based upon his or her everyday experiences. You may like to adapt the title to suit your character: 'Always at Work', 'Always Away', 'Always Second Class'. The poem could be presented as a rap.

A South African Scrapbook

Black against black: Joseph's Story

Sissie:	I've seen this picture before. It's you at work, isn't it?
Joseph:	Yes, Sissie, it is. Working as hard as you should be at your school work!
Sissie:	Why have you lit all the candles? And why have you put in this other picture?

Joseph:	Well, one is connected to the other. There was no electricity in our house, so, when it went dark, I had to work by candlelight. Across our backyard was the huge power station, but it only provided electricity for the white families, despite the fact that it was on the edge of the township.

Black Against Black: Joseph's Story

TASKS

1 In pairs, brainstorm a list of ways in which your lives would change if your homes did not have electricity.

2 Think about how the people in the township who perhaps work at the power station feel about the fact that their homes do not have power and their streets are not lit. In the role of a township resident (this could be Katse, Florence, or another imaginary person), write a letter of complaint to the authorities about your grievance.

3 You follow up your letter with a visit to the controller of the power station. You need to ask why power is not provided and the controller needs to present reasons why it cannot be provided. In pairs, improvise the conversation which takes place.

> SISSIE: But you must have been able to work hard, Daddy. Look where you are now! You are as clever as your teacher was, if not more so!
>
> JOSEPH: Yes ... look where I am now. Here is a picture of me at my fine place of work ...

A South African Scrapbook

BACKGROUND INFORMATION

- Although schools in South Africa are now taking in black and white children, for many years black children went to poor township schools to receive only a minimum basic education.

- Before the schools became mixed, there was one teacher for every 15 white children, as opposed to one teacher for over forty black pupils.

- In 1983, over 1300 rand were spent on every white child's education, compared to only 192 rand for every African.

- In 1979, the percentage of children from each group in secondary school was: white – 37%, African – 14%.

- In 1991, it was reported that for every 10,000 black children that started school, only 113 passed their final examinations.

- In 1959, laws prevented black people from registering at white universities.

- The Apartheid policy clearly intended to limit the education of blacks. In 1954, the government official Dr H.F. Verwoerd said:

> The Bantu [black] must be guided to serve his own community in all respects. There is no place for him in the European community above the level of certain forms of labour.

- Many riots broke out, and students joined school strikes, when the government ruled that instead of African languages, the schools would have to teach Afrikaans only (the white language which has no use outside South Africa). The worst riots took place in 1976–77 in Soweto, in the course of which many student demonstrators were killed by the police.

- Riots have broken out more recently over the overcrowding in black schools. While some white schools have stood empty because of falling numbers of pupils, black children have been taught in classes of over fifty because of lack of resources. The ANC led marches to protest at this situation, as the following newspaper stories explain.

Black Against Black: Joseph's Story

ANC targets the school crisis

[…] It is with much distress that people in the black townships have noted the government's policy of late of closing down white schools in white areas for lack of white children and then failing to make these pristine school buildings available to black children.

The vastly overcrowded township of Alexandra, on the periphery of Johannesburg's most affluent white suburbs, suffers from as chronic a lack of educational facilities as anywhere else. So it was with dismay that news reached the township that a white school four miles down the road in Orange Grove had been closed down and offered for sale to the Jewish Board of Deputies.

So the pro-ANC National Education Crisis Committee (NECC) organised a plan to send 300 Alexandra students to occupy the Orange Grove school. They were gathered ready to go when the police and army stepped in and stopped the students from entering Alexandra.

From Pretoria the minister responsible for black education, Stoffel van der Merwe, weighed in with rhetoric if anything more ham-fisted, saying that teachers who joined the march would not be paid and that pupils who took part would not be supplied with books.

(*The Independent*, 30 July 1991)

A South African Scrapbook

Police shoot dead school protest boy

Police shot dead a black boy, aged 14, and wounded five yesterday at the start of a week-long school boycott led by the African National Congress.

Police at Standerton, south-east of Johannesburg, opened fire on black pupils who were throwing rocks at a secondary school and demanding that teachers leave the building.

A police spokesman said that when the children were asked to disperse they began throwing rocks at police. 'The members fired a number of shots with shotguns and a 9mm pistol to deflect the attack,' he said.

Dr Stoffel van der Merwe, Education Minister, warned that the government would take firm action if the ANC went ahead with plans today to occupy three whites-only schools in Johannesburg with thousands of black pupils.

The schools have been closed because of a reduction in the number of white schoolchildren.

Dr van der Merwe said the ANC's actions made no sense when the government and the ANC were negotiating to iron out injustices in the education system.

The ANC wants empty white schools to be opened to blacks to ease overcrowding in black township classrooms.

But its major demand is that the government must introduce a unitary education system for all South Africans.

Dr Van der Merwe said it was particularly disturbing that the ANC was using children as cannon-fodder to attain policital ends.

[…]

(by Fred Bridgland, *The Daily Telegraph*, 21 August 1991)

The following extract from *Waiting for the Rain* reveals something of white South Africans' attitudes towards black education. Here, the news reaches the baas that Tengo wishes to leave his farm and go to school in the township.

'It's Tengo, Madam.'
'Tengo! Is he up to no good? If he's in trouble with the law, we can't help you, you know.'
'No, Madam. Tengo is a good boy. He wouldn't do anything wrong. No, Madam. He is driving us mad. He wants to go away from here – from the farm. He wants to go to school. That is all we hear from him, night and day, day and night.'
'School! Why, isn't he happy on the farm? We treat him well. He has a full stomach.'

'No, Madam. You and the oubaas, you are very kind. It's not that. He is a clever boy, and he has always wanted to learn, to study. But since my Zinsi went away to school and got sick and died – and that was not so long after we lost our baby – I am afraid to let him go.'

'Why should you be afraid? The school at Boesmanskloof isn't far. He could go there and come home at weekends.'

'No, Madam. He doesn't want to go there. His cousins have told him it is a very poor school. He wants to go to school in Johannesburg.'

'Johannesburg!' madam said. 'The child must be mad. Does he have any idea what is going on there? The township is a terrible place – filthy and full of criminals. And now agitators are making trouble there all the time, stirring up unrest so that the police have to come in to try and quieten things down.'

'I know, Madam,' Selina said. She sighed deeply and shook her head. 'Timothy and I, we are telling him this all the time ... every day. But he says if his cousins – Joseph and the others – are managing to go to school there, he can too. Joseph is a very good student; he is getting ready to write his matriculation exam. And this is what Tengo wants also.'

'So what are you going to do, Selina?'

'I have written to my sister in Johannesburg. She and my brother and his wife and his mother-in-law, they have a house in the township. I've written to ask if Tengo can come and stay with them and go to school. But oh, Madam – my heart, it is very heavy.'

'The master is not going to be pleased to hear this, Selina. After all the expense, and the training Tengo has had on the farm. He's worried enough about the drought.'

'I'm sorry, Madam.'

'Do you want the master to try and talk some sense into Tengo?'

'It won't help, Madam. His mind is made up.'

'Well –' She mopped her upper lip with her handkerchief. 'I'm sorry for your trouble, Selina – but I don't want any more china smashed.' She went back out onto the step, lowered her bulk into the creaking wicker chair, and took up her embroidery again, a look of displeasure on her flushed, heated face.

At dinner that evening, Selina came into the dining room with a tray. She set it down on the sideboard and brought the dishes of food to the table. The oubaas took up the carving knife and steel and sharpened the blade edge. 'So, Selina –' With precision his great thick-fingered hands carved thin slices of white meat off the chicken breast.

'What's this nonsense I hear about Tengo wanting to go to school in Johannesburg?'

'It is so, Master. Timothy and I, we are very worried about letting him go, but it's no use. He says if we won't let him go, he'll go without our permission.'

'Maybe a good hiding is what he needs to shake all that nonsense out of him.'

Selina remained silent, the tray in her hand.

The madam served cabbage and boiled potatoes onto their plates.

'Has he ever been to the township, Selina?'

'No, Master. He has never been to Johannesburg.'

The oubaas gave a short laugh. 'Don't worry then. He'll give the place one look and come running back to the farm, I promise you. I wouldn't worry myself too much about him remaining there if I were you, Selina.'

'Yes, Master.' She went back to the kitchen.

Tant Sannie cut open a potato on her plate, waited for it to cool. 'I knew it would come to no good when those boxes of books came.' She speared a piece of potato onto her fork and blew on it. 'Filling his head up with ideas not suitable for a kaffir ...' She placed the potato in her mouth and exuded its heat through pursed lips. 'He used to be a perfectly willing piccanin before that.'

'So long as a native knows his place he'll be all right.' Oom Koos laid a couple of slices of the brown meat he knew she loved on her plate. 'But once he starts getting ideas, he no longer knows his place – and then you get trouble. That's the reason for all the unrest they're having in the townships. I tell you, Sannie, when I was a boy growing up here on the farm, you would never have heard of a kaffir wanting to read and write.' He poured gravy from the sauce boat over his food. [...]

from *Waiting for the Rain* by Sheila Gordon

QUESTIONS *to think and talk about*

- Why is education important? How could a good education change your life?
- How could a differing standard of education for black and white children help to support Apartheid?

- Why do you think that the Africans objected so strongly to being taught in Afrikaans?
- Do you think that there are any similarities between the attitudes expressed in H.F. Verwoerd's speech on p.62 and the oubaas's words in the story extract?
- What does the oubaas think Tengo's real value is?

TASKS

1 Look carefully at the picture of Joseph's school (p.61). In pairs, imagine that you have applied for a job as a teacher there. What questions would you need to ask about the school before you went for an interview and had to decide whether or not to take the job? Jot down all the questions you would ask during a visit to the school.

Your teacher will take the role of Joseph, the Principal of the school. As a group of candidates, put your questions to him about his school, and about the job for which you are applying.

The candidates are left to chat to the students in the school. Decide which role you are going to take. The candidates now circulate among the pupils and ask them about their school and its facilities. What do the students have to say?

2 Using the picture and the background information on education for blacks on pages 61–62, write a letter to the local newspaper from the point of view of a black parent, giving your reaction to the standard of education provided for your children.

SISSIE: Are these pieces of your old school work?

JOSEPH: No, they were written by two of my students, but they tell the story of one of the most difficult days we ever had to deal with.

A South African Scrapbook

What going on the Township

On Tuesday the police come to our school and they shout two times and they throw tear gases in the shool yard and the children throwed stones to them and they left the school and they call hippos and they soround our school and the principal talked to them and the left the school angry

It was on Tuesday during break we saw many soldiers coming to us. They were muching all the way, and they were having guns in their hands, and the children starting to ren away to school, but the big boys standing near the store calling them say come.

When the soldiers reach the second street they ren away to school. The soldiers came to school. The teachers decide to close the gate. They came to school, talk to the teachers and they ask for us an excuse.

At that time some children are ren to classes some of them the jumping the school fence and they ren away. The soldier decided to get house to house hunting for those who did not go to schools.

Black Against Black: Joseph's Story

SISSIE: Did this really happen, or were the children just writing stories?

JOSEPH: Well, it is a story, but it is a true story.

SISSIE: Why did the police come?

JOSEPH: There had been a lot of trouble with the police ever since the protests about the use of Afrikaans in schools. But the previous week we had been on a march to protest about our not being allowed to use the local white school which was standing empty because there were not enough students to fill it. We wanted to use the space, but the police arrived to stop our protest. I think it was the frustration about that which began the stone-throwing on the Tuesday. Here is my version of the day from our school log book.

Tuesday 16th June
Morning lessons suspended today after a serious disturbance. Attendance was only 62% at 9.00 am with many of the older students absent.

Shortly after assembly at 9.30, many students arrived late, jumping the fence to get onto the school premises. Police patrols in armoured vehicles were in pursuit, firing tear gas, some of which fell inside the school fence. I took the decision to close the gates against the police until the situation could be controlled.

Apparently, some students had been involved in the stoning of police vehicles, and had run to the school for safety. I promised a full attendance check, and the police left to conduct house to house searches.

Attendance check revealed that all the students in school were on roll, and were therefore bone fide students of our school. Classes resumed again at 11.00 am, after an extended break. An emergency staff meeting to discuss our response to the incident will take place tomorrow afternoon at 4.00 pm.

A long section of fencing was damaged during the incident, which will have to be taken down this week for safety until money can be found to repair it.

A South African Scrapbook

TASKS

1   Read the accounts of the incident from the school log book and the students' exercise books. In pairs, talk about the differences you can detect between the accounts written by the students and that written by Joseph. You might like to think about:

– words or phrases you cannot understand in any of the pieces;
– the way in which the incident has been retold;
– any details which are present in one account but absent from the others.

Share your findings with the whole group. Which account did you think was the most successful in conveying the day's events?

2   During 'house to house' searches, the police ask for statements from people who saw what happened. Write an anonymous statement of the incident, based on the accounts you have read.

3   Think carefully about the conversation which is reported to have taken place when the principal talked to the police. In pairs, improvise the conversation which took place that day between Joseph and the police chief at the school gates. What reasons can Joseph find for the police officers' actions?

4   Back inside the school, Joseph speaks to some of the students who, the police claimed, were involved in the earlier stoning. Swap partners, and improvise this conversation. Are the versions of events different in any way?

5   In pairs, using the information you have gathered in the improvisations so far, write statements on the incident from the police officers' and the school students' point of view. How do they compare?

6   At an emergency staff meeting, the teachers meet to share the information they have gathered from the students and the police. What action do they decide to take? What are their options, now that the police are surrounding the school?

7   Think about how your own lives contrast with those of the students in the township. Write your own diary of events in school entitled 'Last Tuesday'. Try to include the very best and very worst thing that happened to you, no matter how small or silly it seems to be. How does your piece of writing differ from those on p. 68?

> SISSIE: It must have been very frightening. Was there nothing you could do?
> JOSEPH: Well, there was wrong on both sides, Sissie, and there was little I could do. But I wanted to make a point, so I wrote to the paper about it.
> SISSIE: But there are two letters here. What does the other one say?

Black Against Black: Joseph's Story

Thursday, 18 June

Sir,

I am writing in response to your story 'Police Clampdown on Student Rioters' in yesterday's paper. As Principal of the school in question, I feel that it is my duty to defend my students against what I can only describe as excessive, terrifying and brutal police force.

I cannot be responsible for every moment of my students' lives. Whatever did happen on the way to school that day – and I do not deny the possibility that a minority could have been involved in some kind of violent behaviour – is a matter for the police and the guilty individuals to sort out. What I do feel extremely strongly about is the way the police – supposedly our 'officers of law and order' – then went out persecuting innocent children in pursuit of their goal.

All the children at the school cannot have been involved in any stoning that took place. That is clear. Yet during that day, ALL the students at the school were subjected to tear gas attack, baton charges in the streets surrounding the school, harassment throughout the day, and the emotional strain of being caged into a building like wild animals. Many of the younger ones were simply terrified: all were too scared to think about working.

Consequently, I was forced to take the action I did, which was to deny the police access to my students or entry to my school. I am not defending my decisions here, merely pointing out that while the police act in this intimidating and bullying manner, I will not be prepared to co-operate with them in enquiries involving my students, whatever they have supposedly done.

It is true that I have been involved in ANC protests about the poor state of our education. It is true that I sympathise with what the ANC has to say about our situation. But this incident had nothing to do with my politics or those of anyone else – it was to do with the persecution of children who do not even understand politics but who do understand oppression.

I am all for law and order, and the troublemakers in society must be punished, but the means of arrest and enquiry must be fair and humane.

Yours faithfully,

Joseph Mathabe
Principal, Soweto High School

Saturday, 20 June

Sir,

I am writing to you in response to the letter in your paper yesterday regarding the police action at the Soweto High School, from one of our supposedly 'respectable' members of the community – my brother, Joseph Mathabe.

I am not ashamed to publish my differences with my own brother. He has a comfortable life as a schoolmaster, while I have had to fight for every rand I have ever earned, and I am now proud to be the owner of several of our town's most popular bars. If the incident on Tuesday affected him, then it certainly did me also.

My bar 'Meadowland' is on the road to the school. On Tuesday morning, it was quite full with a group of Zulu workers from the hostel next door. These are hard-working, friendly and law-abiding people who often frequent my bar.

Suddenly, a gang of so-called 'students' ran into the front yard, hurling bricks and bottles at the police who were giving chase. In their cowardly frenzy to escape the officers of law and order, they damaged fences and gates. When the police returned fire to defend themselves with tear gas and rubber bullets, the front of my bar was damaged beyond easy repair. The riot caused by these youths will cost me dearly.

As if this is not enough, I then hear that our 'esteemed' Principal will not even allow the police access to the guilty rioters who were clearly seen running into the school, and who were known to be hiding there. They will now be free to cause more havoc tomorrow! How can we ever have a safe society if criminals cannot be brought to justice? If they were ever found on my property, I would hand them over willingly to the police, and if Mr Joseph Mathabe was interested in ending trouble, he would have done so too.

I continue to work hard for my living, and I hope to enjoy the protection of the police in the future against the violence on our streets. I hope that those guilty of the trouble on Tuesday will be caught and punished, regardless of that man's efforts to stop our police in the execution of their duty.

Yours faithfully,

Walter Mathabe
Businessman

A South African Scrapbook

> JOSEPH: It was written in response to mine. I'm afraid it was from a very angry person who had not agreed with my point of view.
>
> SISSIE: Who was that?
>
> JOSEPH: Your Uncle Walter.
>
> SISSIE: Uncle Walter! And there are some pictures of him. It is so long since we have seen him. Why was he so angry?
>
> JOSEPH: Well, he sees things differently from the rest of us. His life has turned out very differently. You only have to look at his house, his car and his clothes!

Black Against Black: Joseph's Story

> SISSIE: I would like to visit his house. It looks very smart, and I bet he has a nice car. So not all houses are as shabby as Grandpa Katse's used to be?
>
> JOSEPH: No, Sissie, for some they are much better now. But you will not be visiting Uncle Walter, I am afraid. He doesn't want to see us now.
>
> SISSIE: Why not?
>
> JOSEPH: Well, it is very difficult to explain. Although we are from the same family, we have different views as to how to change South Africa. The newspaper cutting talks about two groups of black people. I march with a group called the ANC in protest against white rule. Uncle Walter has made his money from bars in the townships which serve the Zulu migrant workers. They belong to a group called the Inkatha. Walter is not of that tribe, but he sympathises with their point of view, and that view is opposed to that of the ANC. We have not spoken for a long while ... that may help you to understand why we said what we did in these letters.

BACKGROUND INFORMATION

- Yet another threat to people living in the townships has been the increasing wave of tribal violence committed by rival black gangs, often reported as 'black on black' violence by the South African government.

- The two main groups in conflict are followers of the ANC (or the African National Congress who have opposed Apartheid for many years and for whom Nelson Mandela acts as leader) and the Zulu warrior group known as 'Inkatha', led by Chief Buthelezi.

- While both groups oppose white rule, they disagree on the way to end it, and this has led to bitter fighting and rivalry in which many people in the townships have been killed. The newspapers are full of such stories ...

A South African Scrapbook

Threat to de Klerk as dirty deeds emerge

[…] But the violence continued – violence described by the government as 'black on black', involving supporters of the ANC and the Zulu Inkatha movement. Between 22 July and 1 September last year, 600 people in townships around Johannesburg were killed. By October the violence had claimed the lives of 4,000 since it began in 1987.

Mr de Klerk joined Mr Mandela and Chief Buthelezi in decrying the violence but little was agreed in analysing its cause. Officially it remained 'black on black violence'. More and more people who had witnessed it in the townships became convinced that it was organised by Inkatha members and carried out by the Zulu inhabitants of the single-sex hostels. The police appeared to stand by and watch. Sometimes Zulus bearing 'traditional weapons', such as clubs and spears, would rampage through non-Zulu areas, killing and looting. There was also a more sinister type of attack – the sudden, apparently random massacres by disciplined groups carrying AK-47 assault rifles.

■ 4 September: 42 died in Sebokeng when the army fired on ANC supporters in conflict with Inkatha members.
■ 13 September: 26 killed in a planned attack on a commuter train near Johannesburg.
■ 12 Feb 1991: 17 reported killed in Natal when a bus was ambushed.
■ 27 March: 13 people died when Zulus attacked a funeral in Alexandra township.
■ 31 March: 19 people died in clashes between the ANC and Inkatha in Natal.
■ 12 May: at Swaniesville near Johannesburg at least 27 died in a raid by Zulu hostel-dwellers.

The ANC consistently blamed the police and demanded that the government act to end the killings. It boycotted its meetings with Mr de Klerk but was forced to talk to Chief Buthelezi, thereby granting him a status it had hoped to deny him. Evidence of collaboration between the state and Inkatha was not easy to establish, however, and was vehemently denied by both.

(*The Independent*, 26 July 1991)

- Many of the Inkatha Zulus are migrant workers who stay in large hostels in the townships which have been the target of ANC attacks. In response, the Inkatha have used traditional Zulu weapons of spears and clubs to attack ANC supporters. The police have found themselves caught in the middle.

Black Against Black: Joseph's Story

QUESTIONS *to think and talk about*

- Read the two letters on p.71 carefully. What are the main differences in the ways in which Joseph and Walter report this incident? Do the accounts conflict in any way?
- Clearly, the two men feel very strongly about the incident; this is obvious from the language they use. Which words and phrases do you think make their attitudes towards the police and the students clear to us?
- Why do you think Joseph calls the police 'supposedly "our officers of law and order"' and Walter calls the pupils 'so-called' students?

TASKS

1 Imagine the last meeting between Walter and Joseph, just after the letters had been published. What do you imagine was said to defend their different viewpoints? In pairs, improvise the conversation.

2 Esther Mathabe, Joseph and Walter's sister (see the family tree on p.4), did not write a letter, but she would have held strong views about her brothers' argument. As a group, brainstorm ideas about Esther's current life and situation. What is Esther like?

3 Using the information you have just gathered, 'hot seat' a member of the group who is willing to take on the character of Esther. What does she think about her brothers' argument, and with whom does she sympathise?

4 In groups of three, imagine that Esther brings the two brothers together to try and make the peace. Improvise the conversation that might have taken place between the three of them.

5 In groups, imagine you are customers at one of Walter's 'Shebeens' or drinking houses. Around the table the night after the incident at the school, the black workers share their views on the police action, and Walter's response. Do they sympathise with their landlord (whose bar has been damaged), or are they concerned about the police attack on black children?

A South African Scrapbook

> SISSIE: This is a bad way to live! Not only are we made separate from the whites, but we are also separated from our own relatives! If it was not for this way of life, I could enjoy visiting Uncle Walter and riding in his car. No wonder the newspaper talked of being 'worlds apart'.
>
> JOSEPH: Indeed, Sissie, indeed. But the sadness is that it is not only our people who are torn apart. White folk are at odds too. Many now sympathise with our cause to be free, but many of their own families – their own people – disagree and wish to stop any change. Even today my paper speaks of the possibility of a civil war.

South Africa quakes at prospect of civil war

The spectre of a white civil war, to add to the black-on-black violence that has claimed 5,000 lives, hangs over South Africa after the bloody battle fought in this small western Transvaal farming town on Friday night between police and members of the far-right Afrikaner Resistance Movement (AWB). Three members of the movement were killed and 56 other people injured, including seven policemen, when 2,000 extremists tried to storm a hall in the town where President F. W. de Klerk was addressing a rally. [...]
(by Allister Sparks, *The Observer,* 11 August 1991)

> SISSIE: What is a civil war, Daddy?
>
> JOSEPH: That is when a war takes place not with another country, but between the people of the same country who draw up sides and fight among themselves over problems in the country. Many people now feel there is so much tension in our country that we too could face a civil war.
>
> SISSIE: It all seems to be so complicated! Whites are fighting whites, blacks are set against blacks, and neither can live together! 'Worlds apart...' I do see what Apartheid means now, but I don't know how we will ever make it better. This scrapbook has just made the situation seem more complicated and impossible to solve!

> JOSEPH: I didn't promise that there would be an answer, Sissie, but to understand the problem is starting out along the right road. There is no simple, easy answer to such a large problem. Unless...
>
> SISSIE: Unless what?
>
> JOSEPH: Well, the book is not finished. It does not contain the story of your life, and perhaps the answer to our country's problems lies in your lifetime, not in the lives which are recorded here.
>
> SISSIE: What do you mean?
>
> JOSEPH: You must keep this book now, Sissie. It is time. Keep a record of your life here in these pages. Perhaps then when you come to pass it on to your children, so that they can understand, the answer to the problem of 'separateness' will have been found. I hope the answer lies in your lifetime. Take the book, and fill up the empty pages, and let us all hope that your life is happier and more fruitful than that of Albert, Katse and Florence. Perhaps then, when you are my age, the newspapers will be telling happier stories than these.
>
> *The scrapbook is closed with a quiet thud, and Joseph places it in Sissie's hands. She looks down at the faded covers, thinking to herself quietly. Silence.*

The scrapbook does not go as far as the events of Sissie's life, and so we cannot be sure what happened to her. The country today is very different from the one in which her great-grandfather Albert lived. The laws governing Apartheid have been removed. There are no Pass Books, no signs for 'Whites Only' and no laws forbidding mixed marriages. Free elections are now being held which provide the chance for whites and blacks to share power. But for some people, attitudes have not changed, and the country's future is very uncertain.

Sissie would have had to work very hard to find happiness, as there are still many barriers to be overcome for black people.

A South African Scrapbook

In Search of Dragon's Mountain:
A PLAY ABOUT SOUTH AFRICA ...

The following extract is from a play about South Africa and the Apartheid system by the writer Toeckey Jones. The play is set in the recent past and, in it, the author examines what lies ahead for the younger generations in South Africa. We are invited to see what problems faced two children, Johnnie and Temba, one white and one black, who wish to be friends.

In this way, the play invites us to think about the possible future for children like Sissie: she is told by her father that the future of the country lies in her hands, but what problems might she experience if she became friendly with a white boy?

In this extract, Temba and Johnnie have decided to run away from Johnnie's father's farm (where Temba's family work as servants). They have just been punished for accidentally breaking a gate and, feeling sorry for themselves, they decide to flee to a range of mountains called 'Dragon's Mountain'. They want to see if there really is a dragon there, as folklore suggests, but what they actually discover is something quite different ...

JOHNNIE: What are you staring at?

TEMBA: Dragon's Mountain.

(*She brushes past him*)

JOHNNIE: (*Following her*) Temba? You aren't upset with me?

TEMBA: Why should I be upset with you?

JOHNNIE: Well ... I mean ... you don't believe all that nonsense, do you?

TEMBA: Of course not. When I grow up, I want to marry a tall, kind, brave man with muscles. He won't be ugly, either.

JOHNNIE: UGLY? ... Hey – (*stopping her*) – You think I'm ugly?

TEMBA: You? What have you got to do with it? I'm talking about the man I want to marry.

(*She walks on, leaving him behind. He flexes his arm trying to find a muscle, then he runs after her*)

JOHNNIE: If you think I haven't got muscles, you're wrong. I'm even stronger than my pa!

TEMBA: Johnnie! (*She clutches him*) I'm scared. Your father is going to be very angry when we get home. What'll he do to us?

JOHNNIE: (*Also scared, but hiding it*) I'll take care of him. You needn't worry.

TEMBA: I'm *really* scared, Johnnie.

JOHNNIE: Don't be, Temb. I'm here. I'll protect you. (*He puts his arm round her*)

(*Enter* JOHNNIE'S FATHER. *He is furious.* JOHNNIE *and* TEMBA *spring spart from each other guiltily*)

FATHER: (*Shouting at* JOHNNIE) You little devil! So your ma *was* right. You did run off with *her*! – (*Gesturing at* TEMBA, *who is hiding behind* JOHNNIE) Your ma said Temba was also missing, but I told her she was mad to think my son would run off with a Black servant girl. (*He grabs* JOHNNIE *and shakes him*) My son? You little ...

JOHNNIE: Pa, we only ...

FATHER: (*Threateningly*) Not one word out of you, you hear? Nothing you try to say can make up for the wrong you've done to your ma and me this time. Your ma has been half out of her mind with worry, and I've wasted a *whole* day searching for you.

JOHNNIE: I'm sorry, Pa.

FATHER: *I'm* sorry. Heckuva sorry that I've let you run wild on the farm with Black servant children for so long. You've obviously forgotten how a civilised White boy is supposed to behave. Just as soon as I can fix it, you're going to boarding school, my boy. I'll find the right school that will knock some sense into you. (*To* TEMBA, *who has started edging away*) Hey! Who said you could go? Come back here. I've got something to say to you too.

JOHNNIE: Let her go, Pa. She's done nothing. She wasn't even with me. I only bumped into her a few minutes ago as I was ...

FATHER: (*Slapping* JOHNNIE) You little liar!

TEMBA: Please! My father will be waiting for me.

FATHER: Ya, he will. And you can tell him from me he's fired. I want you and your whole family off my farm by the morning.

JOHNNIE: Pa! You can't ...

FATHER: (*Pushing him*) I've had enough of your lip. You go straight to the house. *Now!* Your ma, at least, needs to know that you're safe. *Go!*

(*He shoves* JOHNNIE *away. But* JOHNNIE *dodges back round him, and stands protectively in front of* TEMBA)

TEMBA: (*Begging*) Please don't make my family leave the farm. This is our home.

FATHER: (*To* JOHNNIE) I said *go to the house!*

(*He grabs* JOHNNIE *who manages to slip* TEMBA *his beloved penknife before he is dragged off by his* FATHER)

FATHER: (Over his shoulder to TEMBA) Don't let me find your family still here in the morning.

(JOHNNIE *is dragged off by his* FATHER. TEMBA *stares after them. She is trembling so much she drops the knife. She picks it up, dusts it off, wraps it carefully in her handkerchief and tucks it into the pocket next to her heart. Then, with a look of terror on her face, she sets off home. She walks more and more slowly until, finally, she stops and stands motionless, with her head buried in her hands. Enter* TEMBA'S MOTHER.)

TEMBA'S MOTHER: Temba?

TEMBA: (*Makes no response*)

MOTHER: Temba! Where have you been all this time? I was so worried. And your baby sister was crying, crying, crying. And I couldn't do the washing because you didn't fetch me any water. And then the Baas came here, looking for Johnnie. Temba, you've been with Johnnie, haven't you? HAVEN'T YOU?

TEMBA: (*Nods, keeping her face hidden*)

MOTHER: *Temba!* I told you to stay away from that boy. You know the Baas don't like him to play with you. I told you no good would come of it. The Baas will be very cross now. Did you see the Baas, Temba? *Temba, talk to me*!

TEMBA: (*Bursting into tears*) Mama ... The Baas says ... we've got to go.

MOTHER: (*Shocked*) Go? *Go?* What do you mean, *Go?*

TEMBA: I'm so sorry, Mama. It's all my fault. I only went with Johnnie to look for the dragon. But the Baas caught us when we were coming back. And he said I must tell Papa he can't work here any more, and we must all leave our house, Mama. The Baas said we must be off the farm by the morning. And it's all my fault, Mama. I'm so sorry.

MOTHER: (*Looks at her in horror*)

TEMBA: What will happen to us now, Mama?

MOTHER: (*hugs her*) ... It'll be all right, my child. It'll be all right. We'll find something. Maybe we'll find a better place than this. And we've still got each other.

TEMBA: Yes, Mama.

(*Exit* TEMBA *and* MOTHER.)

(APARTHEID *comes on briskly and strides to the front of the stage.*)

APARTHEID: (*To the audience*) Ya, it's me. Apartheid! This is my cue. (*Pointing backstage*) They've told me Apartheid takes over the play from now on. About time too! I've been watching just the last bit, and I saw what's-their-names? ... Johnnie and Temba – ya, Johnnie and Temba – coming home from somewhere, and they looked very pally. (*Crossly*) I didn't like that. I didn't like that at all. (*Brightening*) But its okay. Johnnie's father has put a stop to that silly nonsense. He's obviously a good man, Johnnie's father. He thinks like I do. Of course he does. He was brought up under Apartheid. I taught him what to think, by making sure he only learned in school what I wanted him to learn, and only read what I wanted him to read, and only saw programmes on television that I wanted him to see. (*Proudly*) I try to do the same for all my White people. I get into their brains and make them think like I do, because I know what's best for them. (*Pauses and thinks*) I look after my Black people too. They must learn that they're not the same as White people, and can't have the same rights. I know what's best for all my people. (*He glares threateningly at the audience then smiles*) And now Johnnie is being sent to one of my government boarding schools, and he'll learn to agree with Apartheid as well – you'll see!

I'm sure the headmaster will say what I want him to say to Johnnie. But just to make certain, hey, I'll be watching from the wings.

(*Exit* APARTHEID.)

QUESTIONS *to think and talk about*

- What do you make of Johnnie and Temba's relationship from reading the first section of the extract, up to the entrance of Johnnie's father?
- Temba is black, and Johnnie is white. They run away because they have broken a gate by accident. Do you think it is likely that they would be punished in the same way for this? Do they have different reasons for being afraid? Does Temba seem to react differently to the prospect of being caught?
- Read again what happens when Johnnie's father enters. What kind of man do you think he is? How would you describe him? Try to pick out any words, actions or lines which you think might support your view.
- What sort of woman is Temba's mother? How is her reaction to their running away different from Johnnie's father's?
- Look carefully at the words used by (a) Johnnie's father to describe Temba and her family and (b) Temba and her mother to describe Johnnie's father. What do these words tell you about the way in which the people in this scene view each other?
- At the end, Apartheid enters to comment on the scene as an actual character. How effective do you think this is? Does it seem a good idea to you? Share your thoughts about the concept of presenting an *idea* as a *person*. (You might like to talk about the line 'I get into their brains and make them think like I do'.) What do you think is meant by this?

The extract raises many questions for discussion, but it must not be forgotten that a play is written to be performed, not just to be talked about! We know what this play is about – its **content** – but it is not yet clear how that content should be presented to the audience, in other words, what **form** the performance of the play should take.

The following tasks will help you to decide how you can use the extract to make clear to your audience what you already know about Apartheid. Your aim should be to get your audience thinking as they watch – not just sitting and staring!

TASKS

1 Before you consider the extract as a whole, break it up into smaller parts:

Father's opening speech

In small groups, practise a reading of this section, deciding which words need to be stressed in the exchange. Advise the actor playing the part of the father how these words can be made to stand out for your audience.

Temba's conversation with her mother

In small groups, practise a reading of this scene. Think how this scene makes you feel. If you are not reading, try to advise the actors how they can use particular words to make this feeling clear.

2 What words would you use to describe the **mood** or the **feeling** of the two parts of the extract you have worked on above? You now need to consider the use of movement within the acting space to accompany the reading. How close will the actors be to each other? Will they touch at any point? What gestures might be used to show how they feel?

3 In order to try and capture the mood of the scene, direct two or three actors in your group in a tableau of a moment from each scene. Try moving quickly from one tableau to the next. How can you use the different poses to show how the characters feel about each other in the two scenes?

4 When we are angry or upset, we tend to think of things we would like to say which we often keep to ourselves!

Reread the scenes again, but this time allow the actors time to utter any thoughts their character might be having, but which the other actors cannot hear. (For example, what is Temba really thinking when she says, 'Please! My father will be waiting for me.')

5 Reread Apartheid's speech. Here is an idea posing as a character, but how might Apartheid look on stage?

A South African Scrapbook

- Think how you might dress and make up the character for a performance, and sketch your ideas out on paper.

- Think how Apartheid might move on the stage (if at all) and how he might deliver this speech. Having decided which words should be stressed, direct a member of your group in a reading of this speech. (You might like to compare your ideas with those of other groups.)

6 Think back to the stories, scenes and events you have explored in this book. If Apartheid could have been present in any one of these scenes as a character, how might the other characters have reacted to him? Improvise any scene you wish in which Apartheid takes part as a person.

7 The technique of making an idea (or anything non-living) into a person is called *personification*. You know what values Apartheid might have, but what of other 'ideas' which might not agree with Apartheid? Think of another idea which you could 'personify' in a scene, such as 'justice', 'peace', or even 'anger' or 'revenge'. How might this personification answer Apartheid in the scene? Improvise a conversation between the two characters.